The Magik of
Freya and Frigg
Embracing the Goddess Divine of Norse Magik

David Thompson

The Magik of
FREYA AND FRIGG
Embracing the Goddess Divine of Norse Magik

David Thompson

TRANS MUNDANE
PUBLISHING
Occult Knowledge

To All the People who love working magik but hate the silliness that often comes with it.

"Follow my lead, and march onward!" - Freya (according to myth)

Table of Contents

FOREWORD

Hello gentle readers!

This book is a slight departure from my previous works, in that I am now venturing forth to explore the powerful deities of the Norse mythologies. Thus, this book focuses on the Norse Goddesses.

I'd also promised myself, and others on my FB group, that my next book would be a bit shorter than my last book. This book only accomplishes the reverse. It's longer than I had anticipated. The world of Freya and Frigg, essentially sister goddesses, is far more complex to fit into a shorter book. What was eight chapters turned into fifteen, not counting this Note and the following Introduction.

Unless you are already into magik and the Norse Gods and Goddesses, your first exposure might have been comic books and popular movies. Certainly, Thor is quite popular as an action hero. But the character Thor of the movies and comics is a far cry from the actual deity Thor.

I am personally drawn towards goddess magik, the feminine divine. Thus, this particular book is about two of the most fascinating goddesses I have ever worked with, Freya and Frigg, or Frigga. We need to begin from the understanding that these goddesses, like ALL powerful beings, contain multiple aspects. Unlike feminine daemons, these feminine spirits do not have "baneful" aspects, but they can be used for powerful magik for which the outcome isn't as nice as some outcomes.

If you have been in any online groups on magik, or Wicca, or the assorted types of groups, you'll be at least familiar with these goddesses, probably more with Freya than Frigg. Although, depending on which sources you read, these two goddesses can be considered aspects of the same being. For me, they're quite separate. The day Friday is named after Freya. This day can be seen as an auspicious time for conducting rituals and spells related to Freya's domains. Freya is also closely associated with the northern lights and love and beauty. In this way, Freya is very close to Aphrodite. When I summon Freya, the energy is very similar, but with a sharper edge.

Frigg, or Frigga, is a close match energetically to Freya, with some key differences. Such as magik for knowledge and wisdom (Knowledge means you know tomatoes are a fruit.

Wisdom means you don't put tomatoes in a fruit salad. Ketchup then could also be considered a smoothie.) Freya and Frigg are both revered figures in Norse mythology, they embody divine femininity with distinct nuances in their mythological roles.

Both goddesses are deeply connected to aspects of magik and wisdom. Freya, known for her expertise in Seidr, a form of Norse magik, is celebrated for her prophetic abilities. In contrast, Frigg, although less directly tied to magik, exudes an aura of foresight and wisdom. Their association with love, fertility, and birth further intertwines their mythological identities. Freya, particularly, is renowned as a goddess of love and fertility, while Frigg also embodies motherhood and domesticity.

Despite these similarities, they diverge in several aspects. Freya's realm encompasses war and death, distinctively leading the Valkyries and selecting half of the slain warriors for her hall, Folkvangr. Frigg, conversely, is devoid of such martial connections. In their personal lives, Freya's independence is marked by her marriage to Óðr and various romantic liaisons, while Frigg is portrayed as a devoted wife and mother, emphasizing her role in domestic spheres. Freya's influence spans across love, beauty, fertility, gold, sorcery, war, and death, highlighting her multifaceted nature. Frigg, in contrast, focuses more on wisdom and protection as a mother and spouse. As the "queen" of the Aesir, Frigg's status contrasts with Freya's belonging to the Vanir, representing different facets of Norse cosmology and spiritual life. These differences and similarities between Freya and Frigg not only illustrate the diversity within Norse mythology but also offer rich insights for exploration in magik practices and literary compositions.

As with my other books, I spent some time in meditation, making contact with both goddesses and gathering information directly from them, as well as from mythological sources. Seeing how my methods of working magik can be used within the framework of Norse magik. And like my other books, I'll present practical rituals and pathworking methods to allow you to get their magik to actually work.

As in my other High Magik books, each ritual will be as simple as I can make it and allow it to still be effective and powerful. Our subconscious is where magik actually occurs, and sometimes elaborate rituals are a key factor in making our subconscious minds pay attention. *Oh,* subconscious might think, *look at all this ceremony and all these tools, this has to be important!* Humans need ritual, from the time we're infants up until we're ready to shuck off this mortal body and translate into the nonphysical realms.

Introduction

With the echoes of ancient Norse whispers guiding us, we stand at the threshold of a revered tradition, where the powerful goddesses Freya and Frigg reign supreme. The impact that they have is not only evident in the stories of the past, but it reverberates powerfully in the current realm of magik. Understanding the importance of meaning, connection, and transformation in our modern quest can unlock a trove of spiritual depth and practical empowerment.

As we venture into the world of Norse magik, we are not merely dusting off old myths; we are reviving a living tradition that breathes, evolves, and resonates with the beats of our daily lives. At the heart of this resurgence are Freya and Frigg, whose attributes and stories are more than just tales of old. They are vivid maps, rich with symbols and signs that guide the practitioner towards a harmonious and empowered life.

Freya, often depicted with her chariot drawn by cats, a cloak of falcon feathers, and a passion for love and fertility, is not just a deity of affluence but a symbol of the unbridled force of life itself. She embodies the essence of magik that manifests desires into reality, that turns the seed into the bountiful harvest. Her magik is that of attraction, drawing to us that which we seek with the gravitational pull of her divine influence.

On the other hand, Frigg, draped in her cloak of knowing, her eyes reflecting the tapestry of fate she weaves, offers a complementary yet distinct path. Her sphere of influence extends into the domain of foresight, family, and well-being. She represents the magik of binding and protection, creating the weaves that hold families together, turning a house into a home guarded by unseen forces.

The contemporary magikal practitioner approaches these goddesses with a dual aim: to harness their energies, to enhance their lives, and to honor the rich Norse tradition from which these energies emanate. By invoking the presence of Freya, one may seek to attract wealth, love, and success. By paying homage to Frigg, one may find pathways to healing, safeguarding, and nurturing.

But why do these ancient figures hold sway in the age of the microchip and the quantum leap? It is because, within every era, humanity has sought to connect with the larger forces that govern the cosmos. Norse goddesses, like Freya and Frigg, offer a link to these forces. They are the embodiment of natural phenomena, emotional tides, and the human psyche's complexities.

Freya's and Frigg's archetypes speak to the deepest parts of our being. In Freya's case, it's about accepting our wants and longings, allowing ourselves to pursue what brings us happiness and satisfaction. Her magik is not just in the rituals or spells we cast, but in the very act of claiming our right to pursue what we love.

Frigg's archetype invites us into the fold of community and connection. Her magik reminds us of the interwoven nature of our lives with those we care about. It is through her that we learn the art of maintaining those bonds and the sacredness of the spaces we share with our loved ones.

These goddesses also represent a balance that is particularly relevant in today's fast-paced and often fragmented society. Freya teaches us to be fierce and assertive in our ambitions, while Frigg embodies the wisdom of looking inward and caring for our inner circle. Together, they form a complete system of values that promote both personal growth and communal well-being.

Understanding the roles of these goddesses in contemporary magik means recognizing their symbols and influences in our daily practices. It means seeing the golden necklace Brisingamen, not just as a mythical adornment of Freya, but as a metaphor for the interconnected nature of all our pursuits of beauty and value. It means perceiving Frigg's spindle and distaff not just as tools of domesticity, but as emblems of the creative power we wield to shape our destinies and protect our families.

The journey through Norse magik is not a linear one; it spirals deeper and expands wider as we learn and grow. Each step we take with Freya and Frigg is a dance with forces that have been acknowledged and revered for centuries. By engaging with their stories, their symbols, and their magik, we participate in a living tradition, a continuum that enriches our lives with the wisdom of ages.

As we prepare to turn the pages of this book, consider it a grimoire, a sacred text that offers keys to unlock the mysteries that Freya and Frigg hold. It is a tome of transformation, ready to guide the practitioner through the intricacies of Norse magik, imbuing them with the power to weave the old with the new, the ethereal with the tangible, and the divine with the mundane.

Therefore, let us approach with reverence, curiosity, and a willingness to be transformed. Let us learn to wield the energies of love and protection, abundance, and wisdom, as we walk the path laid out by these powerful deities. In this exploration of Freya and Frigg's magik, we not only discover ancient secrets but also uncover new dimensions within ourselves, initiating a journey of both remembrance and discovery.

The resurgence of old-world wisdom in modern practice intertwines the threads of Freya and Frigg within the tapestry of Norse spirituality. The vibrant revival that we are witnessing here is not just a curiosity of a past era, but rather a testament to the lasting influence and power of Norse deities on those who are seeking spiritual enlightenment in the present day. To understand this influence is to unlock secrets of ancient knowledge that have been whispered through the ages and to anchor them firmly into the context of today's quest for spiritual depth and practical guidance.

At the forefront of this revival are Freya and Frigg, whose legends and lore pulse with life, carrying vital keys to the mysteries of existence, love, fate, and sovereignty. Freya, with her intoxicating blend of warrior spirit and enchanting beauty, captures the essence of magik's transformative power. Her stories are not quaint myths but are living energies that can be tapped into for empowerment and enlightenment. She is the embodiment of love and sensuality, a warrior goddess, and a master of the mystic arts.

Frigg, on the other hand, weaves a different sort of magik. Hers is the power of vision, of seeing into the hearts of men and the threads of fate. She is the quintessential mother, the keeper of the hearth, and the protector of families. In her, we find a guide for nurturing the bonds that tie us to our loved ones and the warm embrace of home.

The magik of these goddesses touches every aspect of life, from the way we approach our personal ambitions to the way we interact with our communities. It offers a path to those seeking to imbue their daily existence with meaning, purpose, and a touch of the divine. In a world where technology often distances us from our roots, the stories and practices surrounding Freya and Frigg bring us back to a sense of connection with the natural world and its cycles.

Freya's role in the rebirth of Norse spirituality cannot be overstated. As a goddess of fertility, love, and war, she encompasses the full spectrum of human experience. Her magik invokes passion and prosperity, inspires artists and lovers, and empowers those who seek to claim their place in the world. Freya's tales, filled with her adventures, loves, and battles, remind us of the intrinsic power that lies in embracing our desires and fighting for what we hold dear.

With Frigg, we turn inward to the domain of inner wisdom and the sanctity of domestic life. Her magik is subtle, often operating behind the scenes, yet it is no less powerful. It strengthens the bonds of marriage, fortifies the home against unseen dangers, and grants insight into the unfolding patterns of life. In a sense, Frigg's influence in the resurgence of Norse spirituality is the grounding force, the stable ground upon which practitioners can stand firmly while reaching for the stars.

Together, these goddesses offer a comprehensive view of life's dual nature—the vibrant outward quest for success and the introspective cultivation of familial and personal peace. The revival of Norse spirituality, powered by their presence, is a bridge between these two worlds. It is a movement that honors the individual's quest for achievement and the universal need for a secure and loving home.

In their distinct ways, both Freya and Frigg speak to the human heart with its multifaceted desires and needs. Through Freya, we are taught to be bold, to seek out what brings us joy, and to cherish the beauty in ourselves and the world. Through Frigg, we learn the virtues of foresight, the power of intuition, and the importance of nurturing our personal circles.

These are not just lessons from the past; they are vital components of the present, offering guidance and insight to those who walk the path of Norse spirituality today. Their influence extends into modern magik, where the echoes of their voices can be felt in the rituals and rites that seek to draw down their power into our lives.

To embark on this journey through the magik of Freya and Frigg is to engage with forces as ancient as the windswept mountains of Scandinavia and as timely as the quests of our own hearts. It is to join a lineage of seekers, healers, and warriors who have looked to these goddesses for guidance through the ages.

In the pages that follow, the magik of Freya and Frigg

will be unfolded like a sacred scroll, revealing not only the history and mythology behind these powerful figures but also the ways in which their energies can be accessed and woven into the fabric of 21st-century life. This is not simply a study of ancient beliefs but an invitation to experience the living magik of Norse spirituality, a path that is ever relevant and continually evolving, just as we are.

So let us begin this exploration with open hearts and minds, ready to receive the wisdom of Freya and Frigg, ready to be transformed by their magik, and ready to carry their torch into the future, illuminating the way for those who come after us. The revival of Norse spirituality is not a reconstruction of the old ways but a reawakening to the timeless truths they contain—a celebration of life's majesty, a reverence for the earth, and a recognition of our own divine potential.

CHAPTER 1

Norway, A.D. 800.

A village of thatched buildings and small huts spreads out over the rugged landscape, men and women mill about the central structure in the village, a longhouse. With the onset of evening, when the first star of the night begins to twinkle in the deepening twilight, the atmosphere becomes charged with an anticipation that can almost be felt, a sacred energy that seems to pulse in sync with the very essence of the world. The sky turns a deep purple blue, and a quiet descends onto the land.

It is late spring, so the days are long, the nights are short. A gentle, and refreshing breeze kicks up from the south, making the villager's hair move. The breeze carries a note of fresh water, and the smell of damp wood. A river courses its way around the bend where the village lays. Boats of all sizes are pulled up onto the rocky shore, and the work stops as people begin to gather in the center of the community.

The people stand aside as a tall, well-dressed woman enters the center of the village, and strides with purpose to the longhouse.

This is Sigrun, daughter of the village's leader, who is now the village's gyðja, or priestess.

She embodies the essence of the goddess herself, a vision of divine femininity and strength. Adorned in a robe that mirrors the twilight sky, it is a rich tapestry of deep blues and purples, hues that speak of the mysteries of the night and the depths of the sea. The fabric flows around her like liquid night, moving with a grace that seems almost otherworldly. The robe, cinched at the waist with a golden cord, glints in the moonlight, a subtle nod to the Brisingamen's radiant allure.

Around her neck, she wears a necklace that pays homage to Freya's famed Brisingamen. It's an intricate piece, crafted with care and reverence, each gemstone catching the light and casting prismatic patterns onto the ground and trees around her. This necklace is not just an adornment but a symbol of her connection to Freya, a tangible representation of the goddess's power and beauty.

Her hair, long and unbound, cascades over her shoulders in waves. It's adorned with small, interwoven braids, each tied with threads of gold and silver, reflecting her dedication to the goddess of love and war. In her hair, she wears a circlet made of twisted metals, akin to the branches of Yggdrasil, the World

Tree, symbolizing her connection to the cosmos and the web of fate that Frigg herself weaves.

Sigrun's eyes are painted with kohl, dark and intense, reminiscent of the raven feathers of Odin's companions, Huginn and Muninn. This makeup is not merely for beauty; it's a mark of her role as a seer, one who looks beyond the veil of the mundane world into the deeper truths of the universe. Her lips are tinted with a soft red, like the first blush of dawn that Freya heralds each morning.

On her arms, she wears armlets of twisted gold and silver, each a work of art, echoing the craftsmanship of the dwarves of Norse lore. Her fingers are adorned with rings of various designs, some with runes etched into them, others with stones that catch the light. These are not mere ornaments, but tools of her trade, each chosen for its significance and magikal properties.

It is time. She beckons and begins walking towards a glade near the village, as this ritual will be performed in the open, under the night sky. Walking with purpose, she leads the villagers to the open glade.

She stands within the moonlit grove, her presence as commanding as it is ethereal, a conduit between the earthly realm and the celestial domains of the Norse gods.

As she moves within the sacred space, her movements are fluid and deliberate, each step and gesture imbued with intention and grace. She is the focal point of the ritual, a living embodiment of Freya's aspects. In her, the goddess's strength, beauty, and wisdom are manifest, a beacon of divine feminine power in the hallowed grove.

Here, the altar stands, draped in a cloth of deepest gold, reminiscent of Freya's own luminous beauty. Upon it, symbols of her power are lovingly arranged: a replica of the Brisingamen, shimmering with an otherworldly light; a pair of golden candles, their flames dancing like the mischievous eyes of a cat; and a small, intricately carved falcon, wings outstretched in eternal flight.

The air is rich with the scent of vanilla and amber incense, swirling in ethereal patterns, weaving an intoxicating spell that heightens the senses. The fragrance invokes the essence of Freya herself, a blend of warrior strength and voluptuous charm, as enigmatic as the goddess who inspires it.

As the ritual begins, Sigrun steps into the circle, her movements deliberate and reverent. They are the conduit for Freya's energy, a bridge between the divine and the mortal. With each step, she recites an ancient invocation, her voice a melodic whisper that merges with the rustling of leaves and the gentle murmur of the night.

"Freya, Mistress of Sessrúmnir, hear my call.
Goddess of love, beauty, and battle,
I invoke thee with heart and soul,

Bless this sacred rite with your presence."

The invocation is an opening, a welcome to the goddess to partake in the ritual and bless it with her presence. She then takes the Brisingamen replica, holding it aloft in the moonlight, allowing it to catch the celestial rays. In this moment, the villagers focus on their intention, be it seeking love, enhancing personal allure, or drawing strength for life's battles. The necklace is then placed back upon the altar, a symbolic offering to Freya, a token of trust and devotion.

Next, the golden candles are lit, their flames casting a warm, inviting light. Sigrun gazes into the fire, contemplating Freya's dual aspects. The villagers look on. They see in the flames her warrior spirit and in the soft glow, her loving embrace. The light becomes a beacon, calling to the goddess, inviting her into the sacred space.

As the incense burns, its smoke rising in curling tendrils towards the heavens, the practitioner begins a chant, a rhythmic, hypnotic recitation that weaves through the night air. The words are a mix of praise and petition, honoring Freya's many facets while seeking her guidance and blessings.

"Vanadis of the shining day,
Guide me in love's intricate play.
Warrior of the untamed heart,

Grant me your courage, your warrior's art."

With the chant, the energy within the circle intensifies, growing thick with power and potential. The practitioner, now deeply entranced in the ritual, moves in a dance-like manner around the altar, their body swaying to an ancient rhythm that resonates with the heartbeat of the earth. This dance is an act of unity, a physical manifestation of the bond between worshipper and deity.

As the ritual reaches its zenith, the practitioner pauses, standing still and silent before the altar. They reach a state of deep communion with the goddess, their mind and spirit open to her whispers and wisdom. In this sacred moment, they seek Freya's blessings, her guidance, or her strength, pouring their desires and hopes into the magikal space they have created.

The ritual concludes with a final act of gratitude and reverence. Sigrun gently extinguishes the candles, each wisp of smoke carrying their thanks to the goddess. The villagers now leave the sacred grove with a sense of fulfillment and connection, the presence of Freya lingering in their soul, a reminder of the divine dance they shared.

Items needed for the rituals

I have tried to keep the rituals as simple as possible, all while maintaining the powerful connection to these fascinating goddesses.

Grab yourself a set of Runes. Not every ritual need these, but they will assist in connecting to the goddesses.

The runes sometimes associated with Freya are:

Kenaz (or Kano): This rune is often associated with knowledge, enlightenment, and understanding. It can be connected to Freya as a symbol of her role as a völva, a practitioner of the Norse form of magic known as seidr.

Gebo: Representing gifts and hospitality, this rune aligns with Freya's associations with love and relationships. The concept of giving and receiving, which is central to Gebo, resonates with the themes of love and partnership.

Berkano (or Berkana): Symbolizing birth, growth, and fertility, this rune is closely related to Freya's aspects as a goddess of fertility and love. It embodies the nurturing aspect of Freya.

Ehwaz: Often linked to partnership and trust, this rune could symbolize Freya's connection with her chariot drawn by cats, reflecting relationships and journeys.

Fehu: Associated with wealth and abundance, Fehu can be linked to Freya's role as a goddess of fertility and prosperity.

For Frigg, here's some suggested runes for her energy:

Ansuz: This rune is often associated with communication, wisdom, and the divine. It can be connected to Frigg as a symbol of her wisdom and her role as a confidante and advisor to Odin.

Berkano (or Berkana): Symbolizing birth, growth, and nurturing, this rune aligns with Frigg's aspects as a mother and protector of children. It embodies the nurturing and protective qualities of Frigg.

Perthro: Often linked to fate and the unknown, Perthro can represent Frigg's association with foresight and her reputed ability to know the fate of all beings, though she never reveals it.

Ehwaz: This rune, symbolizing partnership and trust, can be related to Frigg's role in marriage and her relationship with Odin, emphasizing loyalty and deep connection.

Wunjo: Associated with joy and harmony, Wunjo can reflect Frigg's role in ensuring the well-being and happiness of her family and her home, embodying the contentment found in domestic harmony.

You will also need a few candles. Most rituals call for multiple candles. Red, gold, black, green, blue, and white will set you up for most of the rituals. For altar candles, I use 3-inch-wide pillar candles and the smaller chime candles for any specific candle needed for a ritual, such as pink for love, green for wealth, gold for money. Why not green for money? It'll work, but I get better results using gold.

Incense. Sandalwood, perhaps a wood smoke incense like Cedar, sandalwood, myrrh, plus floral incenses will work fine.

Decorating your altar area with fabrics suggested in each ritual, mostly gold or green. I only used my generic pentagram altar cloth, and the rituals worked just fine.

A goblet for water, crystals as suggested for each ritual, offerings will usually be wine, bread or honey.

Symbols of the goddess are suggested, but in most cases, you can substitute the sigils I made for each goddess. You can find those in the back of this book, and online for download. You'll need a PDF viewer to make prints of the sigils.

CHAPTER 2

Norse Mythology

I'd like to take a few pages to talk about Norse mythology, which will kinda serve as the backdrop for Norse magik work. This magik is steeped in nature, it's like stepping into a world where every tree, stone, and gust of wind whispers tales of old, each with a rich vein of magikal practice waiting to be unearthed and understood. Norse mythology is not merely a collection of stories from the distant past; it's a vibrant, living foundation that informs and enhances contemporary magik work. It's more than the action movies so popular right now. In fact, the concept from the movies has altered people's attitude towards older myths, to the point even AI chat bots begin to draw upon the imagery of the Norse deities! Go to Midjourney and have it generate an image of Thor, and you don't get the shaggy bearded god wielding a hammer, but the actor from the movies, dressed in his armor.

I digress. Back to real Norse mythology!

The Norse cosmos is intricately structured, a testament to the depth of understanding the ancients had regarding the universe. It is spread across nine worlds, all connected by Yggdrasil, the world tree, a concept that immediately sets the scene for the magikal practitioner. Yggdrasil represents the interconnectedness of all things, a fundamental principle in magik work. By studying the world tree, practitioners can learn how to connect with and influence the various aspects of their lives and the universe at large.

At the heart of this cosmos are the Aesir and the Vanir, two tribes of gods and goddesses with distinctive roles and powers. The Aesir are often associated with war and governance, while the Vanir are tied to fertility and prosperity. Understanding the nature and stories of these deities provides a complex palette from which to draw magikal inspiration and insight. It's crucial to recognize that these divine beings reflect human traits and natural forces, each deity embodying a specific aspect of existence.

Odin, the Allfather, ruler of the Aesir, is synonymous with wisdom and knowledge. His relentless quest for understanding is a model for magik practitioners, emphasizing the continuous search for deeper magikal truths. Odin's experiences, such as sacrificing his eye for wisdom or hanging from Yggdrasil to gain the secrets of the runes, underscore the idea that knowledge often comes at a price, a concept that resonates with the commitment required for serious magik work.

Thor, with his thunderous hammer Mjolnir, represents strength and protection. His battles against the giants echo the struggle against the chaos and negative forces that practitioners might face in their magikal practices. Invoking Thor in magikal work can be a powerful means of safeguarding one's space and efforts, providing a protective barrier against any disruptive energies.

Freyja, a member of the Vanir and a goddess of love, fertility, and seidr (a form of Norse magik), is an essential figure in magik work. Her expertise in seidr makes her an exemplary guide for those seeking to understand and practice magik. She embodies the idea of transformation and control over one's own destiny—key elements in the practice of magik.

Loki, the trickster, is a complex figure whose stories illustrate the duality of chaos and cunning. In magik work, understanding Loki's nature is vital, as he represents the unpredictable elements that can either hinder or help a practitioner's endeavors. Embracing the lessons of adaptability and cleverness can be crucial when navigating the often-unpredictable tides of magikal practice.

The concept of Ragnarok, the end of the world and the rebirth that follows, is perhaps one of the most striking aspects of Norse mythology. It speaks to the cycle of destruction and creation, an idea that resonates deeply with magik practitioners.

This cyclical view of existence is mirrored in the ebb and flow of energies and the transformational work that lies at the heart of magikal practice.

Each of these elements—Yggdrasil, the gods, their stories, and the cosmic cycles—provides a fertile ground for magik work. Practitioners draw on the energy and archetypes presented in Norse mythology to inform their rituals, spells, and personal growth. For instance, by meditating on Yggdrasil, one can seek to understand the interconnectivity of the cosmos. By aligning with the energies of the Aesir or the Vanir, one can channel specific attributes into their life or magikal workings.

Moreover, the runes, an alphabetic script steeped in magikal significance, offer another profound layer to Norse-influenced magik. Each rune is not just a letter but a symbol of deeper esoteric meaning. Learning the runes is akin to learning the language of the universe as understood by the Norse. Runes are used in divination, to cast spells, and to create talismans, each carrying the weight of the cosmos and the power of the gods themselves.

The sagas and eddas—the epic poems and tales of Norse mythology—are more than stories; they are instruction manuals for the magik practitioner. They reveal the character of the gods, the nature of the cosmos, and the potential for human interaction with divine forces. They speak of destiny, the power of the spoken word, and the importance of action—all principles that are at the core of magikal practice.

To engage with Norse mythology as a background for magik work is to engage with a world where the veil between the divine and the mortal is thin. It is to walk a path where every action is imbued with significance and every symbol holds the key to deeper understanding. This approach to magik is not about blind faith or unseeing worship but about the active engagement with a universe that is alive with power, wisdom, and mystery.

This introduction to Norse mythology is your gateway into a magik practice rich with ancient wisdom and contemporary relevance. The tales of the gods, the structure of the cosmos, the significance of the runes—all these are more than just interesting myths. They are the fabric of a worldview that sees the practitioner as an integral part of a magikal universe, where every spell cast, and ritual performed is a thread woven into the ever-unfolding tapestry of existence. As you turn the pages of this book and delve deeper into the magik of Freya and Frigg, remember that the stories you read are the echoes of the ancients, guiding you on your path as a practitioner of magik.

The Magik of Freya and Frigg

Let's meet the Norse goddesses, Freya and Frigg, where mythology becomes not just a subject of fascination but a tangible path to personal transformation. You are invited to uncover the layers of history, symbolism, and magikal practice that these powerful deities encompass. You can expect to learn not only who these goddesses were in the eyes of the Norse but how their energy can be harnessed in today's magikal workings.

Freya, often called The Lady (not to be confused with the Lady in my Fortune book), is a goddess of love, beauty, fertility, and seiðr, the Norse form of magik. Her domains are vast, her powers immense, and the magikal practices associated with her are equally potent and transformative. Through unique rituals designed to invoke Freya's energy, you can learn to draw love into your life, enhance your personal allure, or deepen your connection to the natural world. These are not just simple spells; they are profound engagements with a divine force.

Frigg, the Allmother, is the quintessence of foresight and wisdom, the wife of Odin and the queen of Asgard. She weaves the clouds themselves, an act that symbolizes the shaping of destiny. Learning the magik associated with Frigg involves understanding the weft and weave of fate, and through her, you can discover rituals that aid in seeing potential futures and making wise choices. The methods you will learn here offer more than foresight; they empower you to actively co-create your reality with the divine.

Pathworking—a technique of magikal meditation and visualization—will be a cornerstone of your journey with these goddesses. You will learn to walk the paths of their worlds, exploring the rich landscapes of Norse mythology and the inner territories of your subconscious. Each step taken on these paths is a step towards deeper self-knowledge and magikal proficiency.

The rituals you will encounter are not just about following steps but understanding the why behind each action. When you light a candle for Freya, you are not just invoking light; you are calling upon her fiery spirit to ignite your passion and creativity. When you weave a charm for Frigg, you are not merely crafting an amulet; you are entwining your intentions with the threads of fate that Frigg herself manipulates.

These deities also offer a unique approach to magik through their association with different facets of life. Freya's connection to wealth and abundance can be channeled into prosperity magik, while Frigg's embodiment of home and hearth offers a foundation for protective and nurturing spells. You'll learn how to blend these energies to address complex needs and desires in your life.

Furthermore, you'll discover that working with Freya and Frigg is not a solitary path. These goddesses stand at the head of their respective communities—the Vanir and the Aesir—and through them, you learn the value of community and support in magikal practice. The magik you practice will ripple through your personal connections, strengthening bonds, and building resilience within your circle.

The methods of magik presented in this book respect the individuality of each practitioner. There is no one-size-fits-all approach here; rather, the rituals and pathworkings are templates that you are encouraged to tailor to your circumstances and intuition. As you grow in your practice, you will learn to weave your personal symbols and significances into the fabric of traditional Norse magik, creating a practice that is uniquely yours, yet deeply rooted in ancient power.

Each chapter of this book is crafted to gradually unfold the secrets and techniques of Freya and Frigg's magik. By layering information and practice, you will build a solid foundation in both the theoretical and practical aspects of Norse magik. The insights gained from these chapters are steppingstones to a more profound magikal understanding, one that empowers you to work in harmony with divine energies.

In learning the magik of these goddesses, you are also receiving an inheritance—a lineage of magikal practitioners who have worked with these deities across centuries. You become part of a tradition that honors the old ways while constantly renewing them through personal experience and innovation.

Your journey through this book will be one of discovery, empowerment, and connection. You will learn how to tap into the wellspring of Norse magik, enriching your life and practice with the wisdom of Freya and Frigg. These pages hold more than knowledge; they offer a transformation that comes from engaging with the divine, an experience that will resonate through every aspect of your being.

So, begin this journey with an open heart and a keen mind, ready to embrace the magik that awaits. Let each page turn be a step further into the embrace of Norse magik, guided by the wisdom of Freya and Frigg, as you weave your own destiny with the ancient threads of the Allmother and dance to the enchanting song of The Lady. Welcome to the path of power, wisdom, and transformation.

Welcome to the magik of Norse goddesses.

RITUALS TO FREYA AND FRIGG

As with any other type of ceremonial magik, Norse magik needs a space that is used for rituals. This space doesn't need to be dedicated to magik. I use my basement now, but I used to use the garage, and before that, my bedroom. I set up using an old TV tray table and stored the rituals items in a bottom drawer of my dresser.

When setting up an altar, keep in mind it's not just for making a spirit feel welcome, it's also a way to get your subconscious into the groove of magik, showing it that the magik is real. To do this, in ceremonial magik, we turn to various tools and items which can be used as a focus of our intent.

For Freya, the enchantress of love and sorcery, her symbols are as vibrant and multifaceted as her persona. To work rituals in her honor, one must consider the inclusion of amber, representative of her tears, and gold, echoing the luster of her famed necklace Brisingamen. These elements serve not just as offerings but as conduits for her potent energies, aligning the ritual space with her essence of love, fertility, and battle prowess.

Furthermore, to capture the essence of Freya's feline affiliations, figures or images of cats can be powerful additions, symbolizing her chariot drawn by these mystical creatures. A depiction of the boar, Hildisvini, her faithful companion in the lore, might also grace the altar, embodying the protective and warlike aspects of her nature. For those seeking her warrior spirit, a miniature sword or spear can be laid upon the altar, a testament to her martial dominion.

Turning to Frigg, the all-seeing matriarch, the ritual items take on a more serene yet equally profound character. As a goddess associated with foresight and wisdom, a spindle, or woven cloth, can be placed in the sacred space, harkening back to her role as a weaver of fates. Keys, as symbols of her role as the keeper of the household, can also be included to unlock deeper intuition and understanding.

For both goddesses, candles will be used to honor the light they bring into magik practice, with colors chosen for their specific attributes: silver or white for Frigg's clarity and wisdom, and for Freya, red or green to mirror her life-giving and passionate nature. Natural elements such as feathers, to symbolize their connection to the skies and divination, and bowls of water, reflecting the emotional depths they navigate, would complete the altar, each item a thread in the tapestry of Norse magik.

While collecting these items, you will weave your own intention into the fabric of the ritual, creating a bridge between the divine and the mortal, between ancient Norse traditions and contemporary magik practice. Each chosen object is a key in its own right, unlocking deeper layers of understanding and connection with these mighty goddesses.

Incense can be kept minimal, using frankincense, myrrh, sandalwood or lavender. There are special goddess blends in some incense brands, but I find those to be overpowering with the perfume, and I prefer using resin.

I'll cover rituals to each goddess in more detail in a few more chapters.

Ritual Preparation

Depending on the magik, most of the ritual in this book will follow the same outline as in my other books.

When preparing for a ritual, it's important you have set a clear and precise intention, and this is reflected by the petition. The magik tends to begin during the crafting of the petition, then grows as you collect the necessary times needed, then it's fired off during the ritual itself.

To navigate the depths of one's true will, as opposed to superficial whims, is a journey into the cavernous self, where the essence of desire burns with unwavering flame. In magik, the practitioner must transcend the ephemeral wants that flicker and fade with the mundane world's ever-changing tides. It is a deep-sea dive into the subconscious, where the pearls of profound longing are hidden.

Superficial desires are like the foam on the ocean's surface, visible and transient, stirred by the wind's fancy. They often masquerade as needs but reveal themselves to be but shadows of deeper yearnings. To identify the core intent, one must silence the cacophony of the fleeting and listen to the whispers of the soul. This process requires a stillness, a meditative introspection that peels away the layers of the ego to reveal the true desire beneath.

Consider the one who seeks wealth through magik. This seeker must question whether it is coin they thirst for, or the security, freedom, or power that wealth can bring. Each of these is a distinct flame, requiring its own unique kindling. In my own practice, I have found that summoning a spirit ally for counsel can illuminate the hidden corners of one's ambition, guiding the practitioner to the heart of their will.

This excavation of the true will is akin to the refinement of raw ore into precious metal; it is an alchemical transformation from the leaden weight of superficial wants to the gold of authentic intent. The alchemist must hold each desire to the flame, asking "Why this?" and "What does it truly serve?" until the dross is burned away, and the purest aspiration remains.

When petitioning Freya or Frigg, or *any entity of power*, the practitioner stands before them, not with a cup overflowing with the trivial but with the distilled essence of their will. It is not enough to know what one wants; one must know why they want it and how it serves their greater path. This depth of understanding creates a resonant frequency that daemons and deities alike cannot only hear but are compelled to answer.

In forging the petition, then, one must not merely script a statement but must craft an evocation that resonates with the core of their being. The sigils provided, the incantations spoken, and the offerings made are all expressions of this resonant truth. They are not just tools, but symbols of the deep-seated will that magik brings to life.

Thus, in preparation for ritual, the practitioner is tasked with this sacred introspection. It is a process both rigorous and revealing, and it is essential for the magik to be effective. For it is not the superficial desire that moves the cosmos but the true will, the star within that guides the magik's course.

Since each topic is unique, I'll present the rituals for each goddess in the chapter on that topic. We'll be covering the usual subjects associated with each goddess: Love, family, health, and a unique form of magik, spae-craft - the magik of prophecy and intuition.

CHAPTER 3

Channeled Histories

As with my other books, I like to spend some time looking at the origins of the spirits we're covering, and this book is no different. As with the other gods and goddesses, there are various origin stories and histories. Many of the Greco-Roman deities came about by having been once editorship in earlier eras, such as Persian gods who evolved (so to speak) into the Grecian gods.

There are some theories that the Norse gods, like the Hindu deities, might have been alien races visiting the planet. But my personal contact with Freya suggests otherwise.

Just as Aphrodite evolved from the earlier goddesses in Persia and Sumer, so did Freya. Freya explained to me she was one of the older Immortal masters who went into spirit to assist after one of many catastrophic events to hit humans in the history of humans, and while in spirit, she assisted in helping the remnants of humans to survive the northern areas of Europe.

Her energy carried her from region to region, sometimes morphing into different goddesses, before she settled into the colder regions of the Norse.

Freya and Frigg are insistent in letting their unique energies be known to far more people than they reach currently and have asked me to craft this major book. Their energy surrounds me. It's also fitting that I am writing this as winter descends onto New England. One of the possible reasons the early Viking explorers left here is because our winters are possibly worse than the winters in their homelands.

Mythological Origins of Freya

In the pantheon of Norse gods, Freya stands resplendent, a figure of awe and enigma, the embodiment of love and war, a deity whose tales are spun with the golden threads of passion and power. Complex and layered, she is a Vanir goddess dwelling with the Aesir, bridging worlds and ideologies. Understanding her is to unravel the tapestry of Norse mythology itself.

Born of the Vanir—associated with fertility, health, and abundance—she is Njord's daughter, her influence permeating beyond these realms. In seismic events that shaped the cosmos, Freya, a token of peace in the Aesir-Vanir war, brought seidr magik to Asgard, marking her as a pivotal cosmic force aligner.

Her domain encompasses the Valkyries, the choosers of the slain. In Sessrúmnir, her hall in the lush Fólkvangr, she receives half of those fallen in battle, offering a nurturing war goddess aspect, affirming love and war's connectedness, reflected in rituals invoking her for land's fertility and battle's ferocity.

Freya's symbols—Brisingamen, her necklace, cats, her sacred animals, and the falcon, whose feathers she dons for shapeshifting flights—symbolize her enchanting might, independence, and far-reaching vision. Her legendary exploits, from quests for Brisingamen to underworld descents, provide wisdom on self-agency and the spiritual-mundane connection for magik practitioners.

Invoking her spirit, one taps into a lineage of magik honed by generations of worshippers. Freya stands in modern Norse spirituality as an enduring old gods' power testament, a beacon for those seeking primal force harmony that shaped the Norse world and still resonates through magik.

Each text section connects you to her essence, deepening understanding, and equipping with the knowledge to weave her magik into your practice. Words here guide deeper into Freya's embrace, a journey to Norse magik's heart, where the goddess of love and war reigns eternal.

Freya's essence, from Vanir roots, is an intrinsic bond between earth and sky. Her role in Norse cosmology transcends dichotomy, a balance of creation and destruction reflecting her origins. Her power echoes in Midgard's fields and Asgard's halls, striding with sovereignty that speaks to her ancient roots.

Her journey to Asgard post-war, introducing seidr magik, forever altered Norse spirituality. Her symbols, the Brisingamen, cats, and boar Hildisvini, reflect her multifaceted nature. Freya's magik is transformational, influencing fate and summoning courage for literal and metaphorical battles.

Freya's magik resonates through the ages. Engaging with her lore taps into ancestral knowledge, drawing upon Vanir strength and Aesir wisdom. Her stories, symbols, and being offer a path to understand old Norse mysteries and explore our spirit through her indomitable presence.

Understanding Freya unlocks our existence layers. Her origins, myths, and symbols guide harnessing ancient world energies for those walking magik's path. Her stories guide through time's mists, illuminating paths with her wisdom's brilliance and magikal warmth.

Symbols

Freya's symbols and totems, not merely objects or creatures of idle fancy, are keys to understanding her multifaceted nature, intricate pieces of a divine puzzle that spell out her influence across the world. Here, we venture into the heart of her symbolism, unwrapping the layers that construct her mythos and endow her followers with the essence of her magik.

The Brisingamen, her illustrious necklace, gleams with

the light of a thousand sunsets, its lore as lustrous as the craftsmanship itself. A creation of the dwarves, master smiths who could coax beauty and power from the bare bones of the earth, the necklace is a marvel—a magikal artifact imbued with the ability to amplify Freya's already formidable attributes. To don the Brisingamen is to be graced with an aura of desirability, diplomacy, and a whisper of the divine feminine power that courses through the veins of the cosmos. It is said that the necklace's allure is irresistible, a testament to Freya's own charms and her mastery over the art of attraction.

But the Brisingamen is not merely a bauble of vanity; it is the very emblem of Freya's sovereignty over love and beauty, her dominion over the heart's most profound emotions. The tales of how Freya acquired the necklace, fraught with cunning and desire, serve as parables to the lengths one might go to in pursuit of something truly precious. Yet, the necklace's splendor also makes it a target for those who would covet its power, setting the stage for epic quests and divine conflicts that enthrall all who hear them.

Freya's chariot, drawn by her sacred cats, Bygul and Trjegul, is an iconic vision, stirring inspiration and reverence. Cats, creatures renowned for their independence and mystique, are fitting companions for a goddess whose own spirit is synonymous with liberty and enigma. They navigate the skies with an elegance that mirrors their mistress's own poise, their silken fur rippling like the very waves of fate that Freya herself can read and bend. In the presence of these feline custodians, one is reminded of Freya's dual nature—nurturing yet fierce, loving yet formidable.

The falcon cloak that Freya possesses allows her to soar across the Nine Worlds, a shapeshifter of astounding ability. The cloak, feathers as delicate and powerful as the breezes they cut through, represents vision and freedom. Donning the falcon's form, Freya sees the world from a vantage point of height and clarity, observing the tapestry of Midgard—our Earth—from a perspective that marries the mundane and the divine. Her ability to transform, to embrace the essence of the falcon, speaks to the adaptability and far-reaching vision that her followers strive to embody in their own magikal practices.

Each of these symbols—the Brisingamen, the cats, the falcon cloak—carry within them a piece of Freya's story and, by extension, a fragment of the wisdom she offers. They are more than mere symbols; they are invitations to delve into the wellspring of knowledge that Freya herself has mastered. They urge the practitioner to ponder the complexities of love, the strategies of war, and the intertwined nature of all things. They are totems of power, reminders that the magik Freya wields is accessible to those who honor her ways, who respect the balance of forces she governs.

And so, as we trace the lines of Freya's symbols, as we

recount the myths that they inspire and the powers they bestow, we connect with an energy that is timeless. The Brisingamen's glow, the cats' grace, the falcon's flight—all these point to a goddess whose essence is interwoven with the world's oldest magik, a deity who commands both the battlefield and the heart with a power that is as nurturing as it is fierce.

This chapter, dedicated to the symbols and totems of Freya, invites you to pause and reflect on the profound meanings each carries. To embrace these symbols is to embrace Freya's magik, to weave her energy into the fabric of your life. As you ponder her totems, let them ignite a spark of understanding in the cryptic language of the gods—a language where love and war dance in eternal interplay, and where Freya reigns as the eternal goddess of both.

As we conclude this segment, let each symbol of Freya settle into your consciousness, enriched by the stories and imbued with the power they represent. Let them be the beacons that guide you deeper into the mysteries of Freya, into the embrace of her magik, and let them light the path to the wisdom you seek. With each totem comes a story, and with each story, a piece of Freya's timeless spirit is revealed, inviting you to explore further, to learn more, and to weave her magik into the tapestry of your journey.

Freya's Exploits in Mythology

In school, I loved reading the myths associated with

various cultures. Anyone who's gone through the United States's education system might have encountered the legendary saga of Beowulf. Unfortunately, for my generation, it stopped here until I was in college.

In the Norse myths, Freya's exploits gleam with the luster of a saga that has transcended the ages. To begin, we turn our gaze to the golden tears of Freya, a tale that captures her essence as the goddess of love. The tears she shed for her lost husband, Óðr, turned to gold upon touching the earth, and to amber when falling into the sea. This myth speaks volumes of her profound emotion and the power of her divine sorrow, casting a light on the boundless depths of her passion and the influence she commands over the natural world.

But Freya's tears were not merely expressions of grief; they were manifestations of magik, each droplet a prism through which her potent energies could bless or curse the land. Such was the might of Freya's love that it could foster prosperity or lay waste to fields, a duality that underscores her complex nature.

The quest for the Brisingamen, Freya's famed necklace, takes us further into her narrative of power and desire. The dwarven-crafted masterpiece, laced with enchantments and the glow of otherworldly craftsmanship, was not simply a bauble to adorn the goddess's neck. It was a conduit of her powers, a source of her allure, and a testament to her sovereign status among the gods and the mortals alike. The story goes that Freya, desiring the necklace above all else, agreed to spend time with each of the four dwarves who crafted it, thereby weaving a complex web of diplomacy and seduction that showcases her cunning and strategic depth.

These endeavors are but glimpses into Freya's agency; her acts of bravery and cunning are the very sinews that bind the muscles of her lore. Take her role with the Valkyries, those choosers of the slain, where Freya stands as the foremost, selecting half of the warriors felled in battle to reside in her hall, Sessrúmnir. Here, in the afterlife's lush meadows of Fólkvangr, these spirits find solace and honor. This task of selection was not merely ceremonial; it was an active engagement in the weaving of fate, a magikal process that shaped the destinies of mortals and the very landscape of the afterworld.

Her exploits further extend to the battlefields themselves, where she rode with Valkyries, not as a distant deity, but as a fervent participant in the fray. In these acts, Freya is not a passive figure of femininity or fertility; she is the very personification of sovereignty and strength, an entity that stands at the forefront of cosmic balance, deciding the fates of warriors and influencing the outcomes of strife.

Yet, perhaps one of the most striking aspects of Freya's endeavors is her shapeshifting ability, a facet of her magik that allowed her unparalleled freedom and reach. With the feathers of a falcon, she could traverse the Nine Worlds, an ability that speaks of her mastery over the elements and her role as a protector of her people. It was through this power that she conducted some of her most daring feats, venturing into realms fraught with danger to secure knowledge or to right a cosmic imbalance.

Even her marital life weaves into the grand story of her legend. Freya's husband, Óðr, often vanished for long periods, leaving her in a state of longing and despair. It's said that her search for him led her across the many worlds, an odyssey that brought her into contact with beings and forces that would intimidate even the stoutest of gods. In her search, she bore different names, taking on new identities, demonstrating her fluid nature and the adaptability of her divine essence.

As these stories unfurl, each thread reveals more than mere adventures; they reflect the very essence of Norse understanding of the universe—a place where the divine interacts with the mortal, where the actions of gods have direct consequences on the world of men. Freya's exploits, therefore, are not just narratives to entertain; they are lessons in the intricate dance of existence, where every act of magik and might is a step in the eternal dance of life and death, love and loss.

The richness of Freya's mythos beckons the magikal practitioner to engage with these narratives, not as distant tales of a bygone era but as living wellsprings of wisdom and empowerment. Through her stories, one can glimpse the core principles of Norse magik—the manipulation of energies, the shaping of destiny, and the profound connection that the gods share with the earthly and the ethereal.

The Symbols of Freya

In our quest to comprehend Freya, we are immersed in a world filled with profound symbols and totems that intricately connect to her core being. The symbols that are linked to Freya are more than just emblems, they carry profound symbolism.

The Brisingamen, her storied necklace, glimmers at the heart of her iconography. It is no mere ornament; it's a magikal fulcrum, as essential to Freya as the hammer is to Thor. Forged by the deft hands of the dwarves, its intricate design captures the interplay of light and shadow, reflecting Freya's dual role as the goddess of love and of war. This necklace, brimming with enchantments, symbolizes the unbreakable bond between beauty and resilience, between the allure of attraction and the mettle of a warrior.

Additionally, let us contemplate the awe-inspiring falcon, whose feathers she adorns herself with in order to achieve the remarkable ability to take flight. High above the Nine Worlds, the majestic falcon gracefully soars, demonstrating its mastery of the boundless skies and symbolizing the essence of freedom and a broader perspective. The falcon cloak holds a deeper meaning for Freya, surpassing its functionality as a mere tool. In the same way that the falcon effortlessly cuts through the air, Freya exhibits unparalleled grace as she skillfully maneuvers through the intricate paths of fate and destiny.

The wild boar, her loyal companion named Hildisvíni, stands for fierce protection and the untamed forces of nature. This is no ordinary beast but a divine guardian, offering both strength and wisdom. The boar's bristles are akin to the needles of a compass in the world of magik, each pointing towards truths hidden deep beneath the surface, truths that Freya knows and guards with a protective ferocity.

Additionally, the golden apples of Idunn hold significance for Freya as they represent everlasting youth and renewal. These apples, while not belonging to her, serve as a symbolic gesture towards the interconnectedness of the gods' blessings and her relentless pursuit of knowledge and power, emphasizing the common magical ties that unite the Norse deities.

Now, for the cats. Yes, cats. It's theorized that the Vikings introduced the Norwegian Forest cat to the far northern part of eastern north America, which soon evolved into the magnificent Maine Coon cat. The theory posits that the Maine Coon's ancestors might have disembarked from Viking ships and then mated with local short-haired breeds, leading to the development of the distinctive Maine Coon characteristics over generations.

However, Freya's chariot, drawn by cats, is interesting in

that, in my experience with cats (which is extensive) I just can't see your average house cat behaving itself enough to pull a chariot, but it's a cool image. You see, cats are symbols of independence and curiosity, reflecting Freya's own unyielding spirit and her thirst for the arcane knowledge that she chases across the realms. The gentle purr of her feline steeds belies a deeper truth; that within what we perceive as gentle and nurturing, there lies the potential for fierce autonomy and bold exploration.

Together, these symbols and totems weave a tapestry rich with meaning, offering us a glimpse into Freya's vast domain. They are touchstones of her power, emblems of her majesty, and in their study, one might glean the subtleties of the magikal world she embodies—one where love can turn the tide of war, where sorrow can transform into beauty, and where the pursuit of knowledge is the most sacred of quests.

As we trace the outlines of these symbols, as we meditate on the facets of the Brisingamen, take flight with the falcon, charge with the boar, savor the promise of youth, and bask in the independence of the cat, we begin to grasp the multiplicity of Freya's nature. We start to understand that these are not just static icons, but living energies, vibrant with the powers of the goddess they represent, beckoning us to explore further, to seek the stories and legends where these symbols come to life.

And it is within these legends, these epic tales of love and war, of loss and triumph, that Freya truly reveals herself. For within her stories lies the vibrant pulse of ancient wisdom, the stirring sagas that have been whispered through the ages, tales that continue to shape our understanding of the magikal and the divine. Each symbol, a door to legend; each totem, a step on a journey that promises to unravel the mysteries of a goddess whose influence stretches across the heavens and the earth.

Freya in Myth

When exploring the world of Norse mythology, one cannot overlook the prominent role played by Freya, the goddess of love and war, who stands out as a remarkably multifaceted and formidable figure. The legends she carries are a testament to the ancient wisdom that holds great significance, showcasing the intricate and diverse aspects of existence where love and conflict are intertwined, and where magik permeates the very air that mortals and gods alike breathe.

Begin your journey into the sagas of Freya with the Brisingamen, a tale as lustrous as the fabled necklace at its heart. The story goes that Freya, whose beauty knew no bounds, happened upon the dwarven craftsmen of Svartheim, four brothers of unparalleled skill. They had forged Brisingamen, the necklace that shone with the light of the very stars. The allure of such a treasure was irresistible to Freya, whose very name means 'the Lady.' In exchange for this masterpiece of metal and gemstone, she agreed to spend one night with each of the brothers, a narrative that underscores her connection to love and sensuality, yes, but also her unyielding determination and sovereignty over her own desires.

Then, there is the enthralling tale of Freya's chariot, drawn by two Norwegian Forest Cats, large and strong enough to bear the weight of a goddess. These cats, Bygul and Trjegul, are more than mere pets; they are totems, representing the dual aspects of Freya's domain—love, denoted by the gentle purring felines, and war, symbolized by their fierce claws and large, muscular builds. The sight of Freya's chariot thundering across the skies, cats in tow, would stir the hearts of all who witnessed it, reminding them of the untamed force of nature that is both nurturing and devastating.

Freya's martial prowess is not to be overshadowed by her beauty. In the tales, she is a Valkyrie, a chooser of the slain, leading the Valkyries in collecting the souls of the most valiant warriors felled in battle. Half of these fallen heroes are welcomed into her hall, Sessrúmnir, a place of honor and merriment, equal to Odin's Valhalla. Her role here exemplifies a bridge between life and death, underscoring her dominion over not only the heart's passions but the finality of death and the glory of valor.

Yet it is not only the bravest warriors who capture Freya's interest. Her exploits with the trickster god Loki reveal a more intricate layer of her persona. In one account, Loki, envious of

Freya's treasures, transforms himself into a fly to infiltrate her chamber and steal the precious Brisingamen. Freya's subsequent despair and relentless search for her lost treasure highlight her profound connection to the artifacts of her power. Her eventual retrieval of Brisingamen, often with the assistance of other gods or by her own cunning, reinforces her as a formidable force, unwavering in the face of adversity and loss.

Her stories are many, each one peeling back the layers of her character, from her love affair with the human Od, which teaches the agony of loss and the relentless search for love, to her weeping golden tears that transform into amber, signifying her deep well of emotion and the tangible beauty that can come from sorrow. Freya's narrative is as much about her victories as it is about her tribulations, forming an intricate portrait of a goddess whose essence is woven into the very fabric of human emotion and the eternal struggle between contrasting forces.

In chronicling Freya's exploits and endeavors, we do not just recount myths of old; we unravel the complexities of existence itself, each story a thread in the broader tapestry of life. Through her, we learn that love can be a battlefield as potent as any war, and that magik is not only the wielding of otherworldly energies but the understanding of the profound connections that bind us to each other and the universe.

These tales of Freya serve not just as entertainment but as guiding narratives that teach us about strength and vulnerability, power and compassion, and the enduring nature of love and war. Through her, we find the embodiment of life's most profound mysteries and the eternal dance between the divine and the mortal. As you turn each page, remember that you are not just reading myths; you are engaging with the essence of human experience, brought to life through the lens of Freya's timeless saga.

CHAPTER 4

Freya's Magik

Now, let's look at the practical magik one can work using Freya.

The goddess presides over a vast spectrum of magik. She is celebrated as the goddess of love and emotional bonds, her powers often sought in rituals that kindle affection or intensify romantic ties. Beyond the realms of the heart, Freya is also revered as a master of Seiðr, an ancient form of Norse magik. This powerful practice involves shaping destiny and foreseeing the weave of futures through complex spells and divination techniques.

Her influence extends to the cycles of birth and regeneration, making her an integral figure in fertility magik. Rituals under her patronage are believed to assist in conception and enhance the vitality of both people and the earth. Though love and fertility are central to her character, Freya embodies the paradoxical nature of a warrior spirit, offering strength and courage to those in the throes of conflict. Her war magik is said to fortify the will and prowess of those headed into battle.

The goddess's domain encompasses the profound practice of shamanic journeying, symbolized by her famed falcon cloak, which grants her the ability to shift shape and traverse various planes of existence. Such feats imply her adeptness in astral projection and spirit communication, serving as a guide for souls and a mediator between the living and the dead. In her role as a psychopomp, Freya's selections of fallen warriors for her hall, Sessrúmnir, illustrate her deep connection with death rites and the reverence of ancestors.

Transformation and change are equally part of her magikal repertoire, aiding those who seek personal evolution or must adapt to new circumstances. Her legendary beauty and charisma are often emulated through enchantment and charm spells, enhancing one's allure and personal magnetism. Freya's wisdom in witchcraft and the esoteric marks her as an archetypal völva, a seeress skilled in high magik, offering a reservoir of knowledge to those who seek to walk the path of the wise.

Her protective aura cannot be understated, as her favor once gained becomes a shield against misfortune and malice. Moreover, her association with opulence—often depicted with her precious Brísingamen—allows her to bestow blessings of wealth and abundance, her generosity as boundless as her might. In her affinity with creatures, cats and falcons in particular, Freya demonstrates a profound link to animal magik and the subtleties of non-human communication.

Lastly, and perhaps most potent, is Freya's domain over sexual magik. Her sovereignty over such sensual energies encompasses the magikal use of sexuality and eroticism. The raw power generated through such intimate acts is channeled for various magikal purposes under her auspices, cementing her as a multifaceted deity whose magik permeates every layer of existence for those who seek her blessing.

Rituals to Freya

The rituals performed in ancient times were complex, requiring multiple people and multiple tools, such as drums. I thought it'd be educational for you, dear reader, to look at a traditional ritual to Freya.

Norse magik, especially rituals dedicated to Freya, the goddess of love, war, and sorcery, are steeped in the rich tapestry of her symbolism. Each ritual is a complex dance of elements, an invocation that weaves together the material and the mystical, offering a connection to Freya's divine power.

At the heart of these rituals lies the Brisingamen, Freya's cherished necklace, symbolizing her control over love and relationships. A ritual invoking love might begin at the twilight hour, where the boundaries between day and night blur, much like the complexities of the heart. Participants often wear necklaces or amulets that echo the Brisingamen's design, forging a link to Freya's magikal dominion. The necklaces are consecrated with oils infused with amber or vanilla, scents that are said to please the goddess and draw her attention.

As the Brisingamen reflects the dual nature of Freya, so do the offerings in these rituals embody duality. A practitioner might place both a sword and a rose upon the altar, the former representing Freya's warrior aspect, and the latter her capacity for deep, enveloping love. These offerings are not chosen at random; they are symbolic gestures, a language through which the devotee communicates with Freya, acknowledging her multifaceted essence.

The use of the falcon, a totem of vision and freedom, takes form in rituals through feathers and images. Ritual participants may don a cloak adorned with feathers or have a representation of a falcon present, symbolizing the ability to move between worlds—a skill Freya herself is famed for. Through the falcon's eyes, seekers of her wisdom ask for clarity and perspective, for the ability to see beyond the immediate, to the heart of what truly matters.

In invoking the boar, Hildisvíni, which stands for protection, practitioners may have figures or carvings of boars surround the ritual space. These serve as talismans of strength and guardianship. The boar's connection to the earth and wild nature aligns with the ritual's intention to ground the practitioner in Freya's protective energy, even as they reach for her celestial wisdom.

The golden apples of Idunn, which Freya has ties to, find their way into rituals in the form of actual apples or golden orbs. They are symbols of life's sweetness, of youth and rejuvenation. An apple may be bitten into to taste the essence of life or shared among participants, creating a bond, as sharing is a sacred act of community and an acknowledgment of the interconnected strands of fate—a principal Freya knows intimately.

Cats, sacred to Freya, are honored in rituals through figures and images, or even the presence of a live cat. Their independent nature is recognized and asked to impart the same strength of will and self-sufficiency to the ritual's participants. The gentle sound of a bell, reminiscent of a cat's collar, might chime throughout the ceremony, calling forth Freya's watchful eye and blessing.

Rituals to Freya often involve chanting or singing, with the cadence of ancient runic poems. These are more than mere words; they are vibrations that resonate with the ancient energies of the world. Participants might invoke her name and epithets, each one a key that unlocks different aspects of her power—Mardöll, "the sea-brightener," for beauty and light; Hörn, "the flaxen," for fertility and abundance; Gefn, "the giver," for generosity and prosperity.

In addition, seidr, the Norse form of magik that Freya is said to have taught to the other gods, is a crucial aspect of these rituals. A seeress, or practitioner, might enter a trance-like state, often aided by rhythmic drumming, to journey into the unseen worlds and seek Freya's guidance. This practice, which requires an open heart and a courageous spirit, allows for direct communication with the divine, a moment where the goddess's voice might be heard through the veil.

The environment in which these rituals take place is of great significance. Ideally, they are performed in nature, beneath the open sky where Freya's energy is most potent. Participants might gather in a grove, near a body of water, or under the night sky, spaces where the natural world is close and the boundary between the mundane and the magikal is thin.

As the ritual reaches its crescendo, offerings of mead or honey wine may be poured onto the earth or into a sacred fire as a libation to Freya, each drop a golden testament to her glory. Participants might then sit in silent meditation, reflecting on her teachings, feeling the surge of magikal energy they have invoked.

To close the ritual, words of thanks are given to Freya, and the space is cleared with the understanding that while the ceremony has ended, the connection to Freya's power remains. The symbols and totems are treated with reverence as they are put away, each holding the residual energy of the ritual and the presence of the goddess.

Such rituals are not mere performances; they are the

means through which practitioners engage with the divine, harnessing the symbolic power of Freya's attributes to manifest their intentions. Through these sacred acts, they honor the goddess and, in turn, imbue their lives with a touch of her magikal essence.

I'll explore the specific rituals in the following chapters. This was just to get you ready to work this powerful magik.

CHAPTER 5

Goddess Frigg

In the high halls of Asgard, where the Aesir convene and the threads of destiny are spun, sits Frigg, the esteemed Matron of the Æsir. She is a figure of majestic grace and profound wisdom, her very essence woven into the fabric of the Norse cosmos. Her background as the wife of Odin and the mother of gods like Baldr underscores her pivotal role in the pantheon, where she is not merely a consort but a central axis around which the Norse universe turns.

Frigg's significance in the Norse pantheon is like the keystone in an arch; without her, the structure of the Norse divine hierarchy would crumble. She holds the fabric of Asgardian society together, her presence a comforting constant amidst the often-tumultuous affairs of gods and men. To understand Frigg is to comprehend the underpinnings of Norse mythology, to grasp the importance of the familial and the prophetic in a world where fate is a tangible force.

Her tapestry is not only familial but also cosmic, for Frigg possesses profound prophetic powers. Her connection to fate is intrinsic, her knowledge vast, yet she holds her counsel, for she knows the weight of destiny's secrets. Like a loom upon which the future is woven, Frigg's insights create patterns that even the other gods cannot discern. She sees the weft and warp of what is to come, yet she chooses the silence of the omniscient, understanding that with great power comes the responsibility to guard it fiercely.

The relationship between Frigg and Odin is one of mutual respect and deep, abiding connection. She is his confidante, the only other entity to sit upon the high seat of Hliðskjálf and gaze out upon the worlds. Together, they preside over Asgard, their union a testament to the balance of power and insight. Frigg's influence complements Odin's quest for knowledge, her foresight a beacon that guides him through the murkiest of cosmic waters.

Her role as a mother further cements her position within the pantheon. Her children, the Norse gods, are embodiments of various aspects of life, from Baldr, the shining one, whose tragic death foretells the coming of Ragnarök, to other less known but equally significant offspring. Her love for them is as vast as the skies of Asgard, and it is this maternal affection that endows her with a unique perspective on the affairs of the gods.

Yet, as we explore the magik and majesty of Frigg's

world, a cautionary note is struck concerning the complex practice of sex magik. While Frigg herself is not directly associated with this practice, the underlying principles of magik within the Norse tradition—where the intertwining of power and intimacy must be navigated with care—hold true. Sex magik, a path fraught with pitfalls for the unwary, harnesses the potent life forces at play in the act of physical union, directing this energy toward magikal ends. However, when wielded without wisdom or respect, it can lead to outcomes unintended, and desires unbound.

As I looked deeper into Frigg's story, the concepts of love, power, prophecy, and motherhood intertwine, each thread a narrative that invites the reader to step beyond mere observation into active engagement. Her story is not a static relic of a bygone era, but a living, breathing lesson in the dynamics of divine power and the sacredness of foreknowledge. Frigg's background is a canvas upon which the complexities of the Norse pantheon are painted, her significance a beacon that guides us through the fog of history into the clarity of understanding.

This fascinating goddess weaves the fabric of the future with the threads of foresight, her prophetic powers as intrinsic to her being as the stars are to the night sky. She sits with the spindle of destiny in her hands, each fiber representing a life, each twist a turn of events yet to unfold. In Norse mythology, her connection to fate is not a mere whisper among the leaves of

Yggdrasil, the World Tree; it is a deep resonance, the kind that stirs the roots and rustles the branches of existence itself.

Her powers of prophecy set her apart, a gift that allows her to discern the patterns of what is to come. Unlike the oracles of ancient Greece, who would enter into frenzies to divine the future, Frigg's prescience is a quiet knowing, a serene gaze that stretches across time. To comprehend her prophetic abilities is to understand the importance of wisdom held in reserve; for Frigg, to know is not always to speak. She chooses silence, recognizing that the fabric of fate is delicate and easily frayed by the hands of the unknowing.

To the uninitiated, Frigg's connection to fate might be likened to the captain of a vessel who can read the stars: she navigates the currents of time with a steady hand, her eyes fixed on the constellations of possibility. With such an analogy, one begins to grasp the magnitude of her role within the Norse pantheon. Her visions are not the erratic flickering of a candle in the wind but the steady glow of the northern star, guiding the gods and mortals alike through the night of uncertainty.

In the great hall of Fensalir, her abode, Frigg contemplates the tapestry of the cosmos, seeing the interlacing lines of lives and events. Her connection to fate is symbiotic, for as much as she observes its course, she also influences it, her insights contributing to the shifting patterns of the tapestry. She understands that every action, every decision, weaves a new line into this ever-growing work of art, and with this knowledge, she holds the power to alter its course with but a single thread.

As we examine the mysteries of her prophetic vision, we discover that her powers are a beacon in the Norse belief system, a source of comfort and guidance. Her foresight offers solace to those who fear the unpredictability of life, and her discretion teaches the value of patience and the virtue of strategic silence. For practitioners of magik, Frigg's example is a masterclass in the judicious use of knowledge, a reminder that the greatest power often lies in the wisdom of restraint.

Her influence on fate is a dance with the Norns, the weavers of destiny themselves. While they craft the fates of all beings, Frigg's vision allows her to see the weft they weave, and perhaps, in her own subtle way, to suggest a pattern or two. This interplay between the Norns and Frigg is a delicate balance, a cosmic negotiation between those who decree destiny and one who perceives its coming to pass.

As the reader ventures further into the secrets of Frigg's prophetic abilities, they are not merely uncovering the aspects of a goddess but are being led to the very wellspring of understanding that defines Norse magik. With each revelation, one steps closer to the heart of a tradition steeped in the reverence for the powers that shape our ends, as inexorably as the river shapes the landscape through which it flows.

As the queen of Asgard and the wife of Odin, Frigg

stands as a central figure in the Norse pantheon. Her relationship with Odin is not merely that of a consort but as an equal partner in the ruling of the realms. She is the only one besides Odin who is allowed to sit upon the high throne of Hlidskjálf and gaze out over the worlds. This unique privilege signifies her importance and the deep trust Odin places in her wisdom and judgment.

Frigg's relationship with Odin is one of profound depth and complexity. They share a bond that transcends the physical realms, rooted in the ancient energies of creation that bind the universe together. Odin, often away on his quests for knowledge and power, leaves Frigg to preside over Asgard's daily matters. She does so with a grace and efficiency that commands respect from gods and mortals alike.

This partnership is based on mutual respect and an understanding of each other's roles in maintaining the balance of the cosmos. Frigg's insight into the future complements Odin's quest for wisdom. Where Odin is the seeker, Frigg is the knower, her foresight an invaluable resource in Odin's decisions and actions. Together, they form a divine synergy, their unity essential for the well-being of the Nine Worlds.

Frigg's role as a mother adds another layer to her divine duties. Her children are among the most revered in the Norse myths, with her son Baldr being a central figure. Baldr's death, which Frigg foresaw but was powerless to prevent, is one of the most poignant tales in Norse mythology. It speaks volumes about the limits of divine power and the inexorable nature of fate. Despite her prophetic abilities, Frigg experiences profound sorrow, a testament to the depth of her maternal love and her connection to her children.

Her other children, too, are a testament to her various aspects. Each one reflects a different facet of her persona, from the fierce and stoic to the loving and kind. Through her children, Frigg's influence extends across the many aspects of life and death, wisdom and war, love, and loss. They are her legacy, each one carrying a piece of her divine essence into the world.

Frigg's relationship with her children also reveals the Norse understanding of maternal energy. She is the archetypal mother, her love and care for her offspring mirroring the protective and nurturing forces that abound in nature. Her children's fates are intertwined with the larger cosmic events that unfold within the myths, showcasing Frigg's dual role in personal and universal scopes.

The magik associated with Frigg, particularly in relation to her family, is one of protection and foresight. She weaves spells that guard her kin, and her blessings are invoked for safety and insight. Frigg's magik is subtle yet powerful, imbued with the wisdom of a mother's love and the strength of a queen's resolve.

Through her divine relationships, Frigg teaches us about the complexity of life's interconnections. Her interactions with

Odin and her children reveal the multifaceted nature of existence, where love, wisdom, power, and vulnerability coalesce. Her tales are not merely narratives to be told; they are experiences to be understood, each one offering insights into the human condition and the workings of the divine.

In the stories of Frigg, one finds a guide for navigating the intricate paths of life, a source of comfort in times of sorrow, and a beacon of hope for the future. As this chapter unfolds, each sentence invites the reader to step further into Frigg's world, to understand the nuances of her divine relationships, and to draw closer to the magik and mystery of her being.

The Magik of Frigg

Frigg's magik is as profound and influential as her role suggests. To grasp the essence of Frigg's magik is to understand the delicate weave of the very fabric of reality and how it can be influenced through her divine insights and abilities.

As the wife of Odin and one of the paramount deities of Asgard, Frigg's magik powers encompass the arts of protection, foresight, and wisdom. These are not crude powers that bend and break, but subtle forces that shape and guide. Her protective magik is not about erecting barriers but about nurturing strength from within—much like the warmth of a hearth fire that keeps the cold at bay.

In the Norse tradition, every home is seen as a small

universe, with the hearth as its sun. Frigg's magik envelops the home, ensuring harmony and stability. Practitioners who seek to channel Frigg's protective energies into their homes might do so by invoking her name during household rituals, lighting candles to honor her, and maintaining a clean and welcoming space that mirrors Frigg's hall, Fensalir, where harmony reigns supreme.

Frigg's prophetic abilities are as vast as the sky itself. She is said to know the fate of all beings, yet she chooses not to reveal all she sees. For modern seekers of magik, tapping into Frigg's foresight involves practices like meditation, reflective divination, and careful interpretation of signs and omens. It is a magik that requires a calm mind and a patient heart, as the strands of fate revealed are often tangled and complex.

We can also use runes, a significant aspect of Norse magik, to gain insight into their paths, just as Frigg might. Casting runes with Frigg in mind, asking for her guidance to understand the messages they hold, can be a powerful practice. However, it is essential to approach these readings with reverence and an understanding that some knowledge might remain veiled, as is Frigg's way.

The Allmother's magik also touches upon the emotional realm, offering healing and support to those in need. This aspect of her magik is gentle, yet immensely powerful, capable of mending the fractures of a weary heart or soothing the turmoil within a troubled mind. Rituals that call upon Frigg for emotional healing often involve creating a sacred, quiet space where one can feel her maternal embrace. They might include the writing of one's fears and sorrows on paper, then offering them to a fire, asking Frigg to transform this pain into wisdom and peace.

In the practice of Frigg's magik, one must also understand the importance of discretion and the power of the unspoken word. Her wisdom teaches that not all thoughts should be voiced, and that silence can be as potent as speech. In this light, magik performed in Frigg's name is done with a thoughtful mind; spells and rituals are crafted with care, knowing that the impact of words and actions in the magikal space can ripple outwards in profound ways.

Frigg's magik powers are deeply interwoven with the concept of interconnectedness. Her domain over marital bonds and familial ties offers practitioners a way to enhance these relationships, to foster love and understanding, and to repair and strengthen the bonds that time and strife may have worn thin. It is a magik of interlacing one's life with the lives of others in a pattern that supports and uplifts, much like the interwoven fibers of a well-crafted garment that Frigg might create.

To use Frigg's magik is to engage with the world with a sense of purpose and a deep understanding of the interconnectedness of all things. It is to embrace her qualities of foresight, wisdom, and the nurturing force of protection. With each step taken in learning and practicing Frigg's magik, the practitioner moves closer to the heart of Norse magikal tradition, where every action is imbued with intention, and every intention is a thread in the grand design of the cosmos.

To enhance your contemporary magikal workings, I encourage you to incorporate these teachings into your rituals, thus allowing Frigg's ancient wisdom to serve as your guiding force. Through her, learn the art of seeing deeply, of protecting gently, and of understanding the profound tapestry of human emotion and fate.

High Magik with Frigg

The following chapters on her magik all use a basic ritual template. We have quite a few choices when it comes to tools and offerings, but the core ritual is like my other High Magik books. I have tested these, and they work.

As you work through these rituals, I encourage you to modify the rituals to suit your needs. I only included a small cross section of rituals for Frigg, and it's incomplete. These will just be starting points for you, on your journey through magik using Frigg.

CHAPTER 6

Freya and Love Magik

Freya embodies the very essence of passion and affection, resonating with the strings of love and magik, making her a celestial paragon. Her influence extends to the depths of the hearts of not only lovers, but also poets and all individuals who long for the exquisite intoxication found in the embrace of love. When we talk about Freya, we are essentially talking about the very essence of love magic, a powerful and ancient energy that has the ability to both connect and set free, as well as to create and bring about profound transformations.

Imagine a world where every whispered affection is carried on the wings of Freya's falcon cloak, where each gaze laden with desire is amplified by her divine presence. Freya's love magik is as the gentle dawn, caressing the world into warmth and light. Her very name is invoked in rites and whispers when love seems as distant as the stars, and her magik is the bridge that brings it within reach.

The lore of Freya's love magik is filled with rituals and rites, which harness the energies of attraction and union. It is said that to invoke Freya in a ritual of love is to open the heart's doors to the possibility of deep, soul-nurturing connections. This is the art of weaving one's desire into the threads of the universe, a practice that aligns the seeker's heart with the rhythm of Freya's own.

When an individual immerses themselves in the study of love magic under the guidance of Freya, it becomes evident that it encompasses more than just the act of invoking a spell or reciting an incantation. In order to fully connect with the magik of Freya, it is essential to have a genuine willingness to open one's heart and freely give and receive love without any conditions. Additionally, one must also embrace vulnerability as a source of inner strength and recognize that true magik manifests when personal intentions are aligned with the divine will of the goddess.

But Freya's dominion extends beyond the platonic and the romantically sweet; it ventures into the realms of sexual magik, where physical love and spiritual ecstasy intertwine. Sexual magik under Freya's aegis is an exploration of energies, a dance of power that taps into the life force itself. It's about recognizing the sacredness in the carnal, the divine spark that ignites within the union of bodies and souls.

Within the sacred space where love and sexual magik meld, practitioners of Freya's magik are reminded that the act of love is not merely a physical joining but a ceremony of energy exchange. Here, partners become alchemists, their bed a sacred altar, their union a rite that celebrates the very essence of life. The magik wrought in such moments is powerful, transformative, and deeply healing, capable of manifesting desires, deepening bonds, and invoking blessings of fertility and prosperity.

Freya teaches that love and sexual magik are not to be trifled with; they are sacred arts that require respect, consent, and a clear heart. She embodies the truth that every act of love and pleasure is a ritual in her honor, and when approached with reverence, can lead to spiritual enlightenment and profound personal growth. To this I can attest myself - having tried all manner of love and sex magik while in my late teens and twenties. Go carefully. It's not that love magik backfires, or sometimes never works, it's that it'll leave you feeling worse off, feeling even lonelier than before the rituals.

I advise not to target a specific individual, but to cast a general attraction ritual to enhance your attractiveness and to pay close attention to who you draw in. Make sure you are very clear on the type of person you wish to attract.

As we examine Freya and love magik, it becomes clear that her teachings are as relevant today as they were in the days of old. In a world where love is often caged by conditions and fears, Freya's magik emerges as a beacon of hope and liberation. She invites us to shed our doubts and to trust in the power of love, to remember that each act of genuine affection is a spell cast, and that with every heartbeat, we are all practitioners of the oldest and most natural magik known to humanity.

Engage with these concepts slowly, savoring the understanding that love magik is a journey, not a destination. It's a continual practice of opening, offering, and becoming, under the benevolent gaze of the goddess who is its embodiment. In the following passages, as the ink unfolds the secrets of Freya's love magik, let each sentence be a step deeper into the heart of this divine magikal practice, an invitation to experience love as the ultimate expression of magik in the human experience.

However, let's also look at what Freya can help in regards to sexual magik.

Sex Magik and Freya

Freya's energy resonates as the embodiment of both love and battle, embodying a magikal duality that merges the fierceness of a warrior with the tenderness of a lover. She walks the intricate weave of sexual magik with the poise of one who understands its potent forces and the subtleties of its power. In the realm of sexual magik, Freya is not just a figure of passion, but a teacher of the sacred energies that flow through all acts of intimacy.

Sexual magik is a practice as old as time, a path walked by those who dare to harness the raw energies of desire and channel them toward a chosen end. It is magik that binds the ethereal with the corporeal, utilizing the surges of passion as currents to propel intentions into the universe. To engage with sexual magik under Freya's aegis is to tap into a wellspring of primal forces, setting forth ripples that can alter the fabric of reality.

Envision the act of love as a rite, where each touch, each breath, each pulse becomes a syllable in a larger incantation. This is the language of Freya's sexual magik, where the physical communion of lovers transmutes into a dance of energy, weaving intentions with actions, threading will through pleasure. The culmination of this rite is a burst of power, released at the moment of climax, a surge potent enough to cast desires into form.

Freya teaches that to engage in sexual magik is to partake in the divine creative process. It is to shape the future with the very essence of life, merging the tangible with the imagined, the flesh with the spirit. Yet, like any potent force, sexual magik is a blade that cuts both ways, a tide that carries as readily to prosperity as it does to ruin if not approached with caution and respect.

To the neophyte, the realms of sexual magik may seem

cloaked in allure and mystery, but beneath the velvet drapes lies a truth etched in the very fabric of the magikal practice—it demands discipline, understanding, and a clear vision. Missteps on this path can be as consequential as the acts themselves. Without clear intent, the energies raised can become untethered specters, and desires can twist into obsessions, tugging the unwary practitioner into the depths of their own abyss.

The risks are real, and the consequences can reverberate through one's life like echoes in an empty hall. For when magik and desire interlace without the guidance of wisdom and control, they can unmake as swiftly as they can create. The unwary may find themselves bound to energies they cannot fathom, tethered to outcomes they did not foresee. Trust me on this one. And like Lilith, Freya can trigger an obsession in the target of the ritual, so proceed with caution.

Freya's guidance on this journey is paramount. She offers the knowledge that sexual magik should not be trifled with in the pursuit of mere pleasure or power. It should be practiced with a partner of aligned intentions and mutual understanding within a sacred space where trust is the foundation and respect is the law. The act itself becomes a sacrament, an offering to the goddess in exchange for her blessings and favor.

Sexual magik, therefore, is an art of balance, a practice of aligning one's deepest desires with the divine will, and conducting the energies raised with precision and care. It is a sacred communion that, when conducted under Freya's watchful eye, can bring about healing, deepen connections, and manifest dreams into reality.

Offerings to Freya

Before I get too deep into the following rituals, here are some suggestions for offerings to this Norse deity. I made sure to list things most of us can obtain without too much trouble.

Offering something to Freya, a Norse goddess deeply connected with love, beauty, and fertility, can be a personal and meaningful practice. Offerings are a traditional way to show reverence and respect to a deity. For Freya, offerings acknowledge her power and importance in the Norse pantheon and demonstrate gratitude for her influence and blessings.

Here are some ideas:

Flowers: Freya, associated with beauty and love, would appreciate fresh flowers, especially those that are fragrant and beautiful, like roses, which symbolize love and passion.

Honey or Mead: As sweet offerings, honey or mead can be used to honor Freya, symbolizing sweetness, and pleasure in life.

Fruit: Apples or pomegranates, fruits often associated with love and fertility, would be appropriate offerings to Freya.

Incense: Scents like rose, vanilla, or sandalwood can be burnt as offerings. Freya's connection to sensuality and love makes fragrant incense a suitable choice.

Music or Poetry: Given Freya's association with beauty and artistic expression, singing a song, playing music, or reciting a poem, especially if self-composed, can be a heartfelt offering.

Candles: Lighting a candle, particularly in colors associated with love and passion like pink or red, can be a simple yet effective offering to invoke Freya's presence and favor.

Natural Offerings: Bird feathers, seashells, or stones picked from meaningful places can be offered, especially if one explains their significance in a prayer or dedication.

Handwritten Letters: Writing a letter expressing your desires, gratitude, or thoughts and offering it to Freya can be a very personal and meaningful way to connect with her.

When offering something to Freya, it's important to do so with intention and respect. The value of the offering lies not in its material worth but in the sincerity and thoughtfulness with which it's given.

Altars to Freya

Most readers of my books are used to me not providing too much in the way of arranging an altar. I always suggest keeping it simple. In magik to Norse Deities, it's common to have a space dedicated to Freya or Frigg. Keeping the items from a ritual on the altar, while awaiting the manifestation of a desire, is a good way to reinforcing the magik.

By adjusting the items on the altar, perhaps handling the crystals, or lighting more incense, will keep your energy aligned with the energy of Freya or Frigg, thus enhancing the magik itself.

High Magik Ritual to Attract a Lover with Freya's Aid

Having given you enough warning, we now proceed to the magik. As I have cautioned, make sure you understand all the ramifications involved with this type of magik.

Items Needed:

1. Pink or Red Altar Cloth: Symbolizing love and passion.

2. Rose Quartz Crystals: For attracting love and enhancing romantic energy.

3. Red or Pink Candles: Representing the flame of passion and desire.

4. Freya's Symbol (such as a representation of a cat or a falcon, or her sigil): To invoke her presence and assistance.

5. Incense (Preferably Rose or Vanilla): To set a loving and inviting atmosphere.

6. Honey: For sweetening the future relationship.

7. Paper and Pen: To write down qualities desired in a lover or a love letter to an unknown lover.

8. Rose Petals: For attracting love and for offering to

Freya.

9. A Personal Item or Photograph of Yourself: To symbolize who the love is being attracted to.

Ritual Setup:

- Lay the altar cloth on a flat surface.

- Arrange the rose quartz crystals around the altar.

- Place the candles in the center and the incense close by.

- Set the symbol of Freya prominently on the altar.

- Place the honey, paper, pen, and rose petals on the altar.

- Keep the personal item or photograph near the written desires.

Summoning Prayer:

"Freya, goddess of love and beauty, hear my call on this enchanted eve.

With your cat's grace and falcon's sight, bring forth love's light to me.

Guide a heart that matches mine, where true connection can be free.

With rose's charm and crystal's shine, let love flow forth, so mote it be."

Ritual Steps:

1. Light the candles and incense to purify the space and

invite Freya's energy.

2. Hold the rose quartz crystals in your hands, infusing them with your desire for love.

3. Place the crystals back on the altar, forming a heart shape.

4. Recite the summoning prayer with genuine intent, focusing on your desire for love.

5. Write down the qualities you seek in a lover or a love letter to an unknown lover. Focus on feelings and character rather than specific physical traits.

6. Anoint the paper with a drop of honey, symbolizing the sweetness you wish to bring into your relationship.

7. Fold the paper and place it under the symbol of Freya.

8. Scatter the rose petals over the altar while visualizing the love you wish to attract.

9. Place your personal item or photograph in the center of the rose petal spread.

10. Close the ritual by giving thanks to Freya for her guidance and assistance.

11. Let the candles burn down safely, sending your intentions out into the universe.

Keep the rose quartz crystals with you as a talisman of love. Regularly refresh the altar setup as a reminder of your intent and to keep Freya's energy present in your love attraction journey.

Attract a Sexual Partner with Freya's Aid

Items Needed:

1.Red or Black Altar Cloth: Representing passion and sexuality.

2.Carnelian or Garnet Crystals: Stones known for enhancing sexual energy and attraction.

3. Red Candles: Symbolizing sexual passion and desire.

4. Figurine or Image of Freya: To honor and invoke the goddess.

5. Incense (Preferably Musk or Patchouli): Scents that are traditionally associated with arousal and attraction.

6. A Bowl of Saltwater: Symbolizing the womb of life and sexual purity.

7. Paper and Pen: To write down specific intentions or characteristics desired in a sexual partner.

8. Rose Petals or Jasmine Flowers: For love and attraction, and as offerings to Freya.

9. A Personal Item or Photograph of Yourself: To direct the focus of the spell towards yourself.

Ritual Setup:

- Spread the altar cloth on a flat surface.

- Arrange the carnelian or garnet crystals on the altar.

- Place the red candles centrally and set the incense to the side.

- Position the figurine or image of Freya prominently.

- Place the bowl of saltwater on the altar.

- Have the paper, pen, rose petals or jasmine flowers, and personal item or photograph within reach.

Summoning Prayer:

"Freya, goddess of love and passion, I call to you with a fervent heart.

In your power and grace, bring forth a connection deep and true.

Guide to me a partner with whom the sparks of desire ignite,

With whom the dance of passion and pleasure is right.

Let our union be one of joy, respect, and fiery delight,

Under your watchful gaze on this magikal night."

Ritual Steps:

1. Light candles and incense to create an inviting and sensually charged atmosphere.

2. Hold the crystals in your hands, focusing on your desire for a passionate, sexual connection.

3. Place the crystals around the figurine or image of

Freya.

4. Recite the summoning prayer, visualizing your intent for a fulfilling sexual partnership.

5. Write down your intentions or desired qualities in a sexual partner on the paper.

6. Dip your fingertips in the saltwater and flick droplets onto the paper, symbolizing the purification and sanctification of your desires.

7. Place the paper under the figurine or image of Freya.

8. Scatter the rose petals or jasmine flowers around the altar as offerings to the goddess.

9. Set your personal item or photograph near the figurine or image of Freya, linking the spell to you.

10. Conclude the ritual by expressing gratitude to Freya for her guidance and presence.

11. Allow the candles to burn down safely, releasing your intentions to the universe.

Keep the charged crystals with you as a reminder of your intent and to maintain a connection with Freya's energy in your quest for a sexual partner. Refresh the altar as needed to reinforce your intent and connection with the goddess.

CHAPTER 7

Frigg's Family and Love Magik

In the grand tapestry of Norse mythology, where gods and goddesses weave the strands of destiny, Frigg, the Allmother, stands as a protector of family and home.Her unique family magik, rich in warmth and protection, is like the hearth in an ancient hall, providing comfort and unity to those who gather around it. Frigg's magik is not just a series of spells or rituals; it is an embodiment of the nurturing spirit, a force that binds families together and turns a house into a home.

Imagine a household, its walls steeped in love and tradition, where each room resonates with stories passed down through generations. This is the essence of Frigg's family magik - creating spaces where love and understanding flourish. Her magik weaves through the very fabric of familial bonds, strengthening relationships and fostering an environment of mutual respect and care. It's like the gentle but firm threads of a spider's web, delicately spun yet resilient, holding the family together against the challenges of life.

Frigg's domain encompasses the sanctity of marriage and the well-being of children, much like a seasoned gardener tending to a precious garden. Her blessings are invoked for harmonious relationships, ensuring that the roots of love grow deep, and the bonds of partnership remain strong against the tempests of time. She watches over children; her magik a gentle caress that guides and protects them as they navigate the journey from youth to adulthood.

Her presence is like a warm, embracing glow, infusing the household with a sense of safety, and belonging. Her energy can be woven into the very walls of a home, creating a sanctuary of peace and happiness. Frigg's family magik can be brought to life through simple daily rituals - a shared meal where stories and laughter are exchanged, a quiet moment of reflection and gratitude at the end of the day, or a heartfelt conversation where words are spoken and heard with empathy and love.

Frigg's wisdom extends to healing the rifts and resolving the conflicts that inevitably arise within families. Her magik is like the soothing balm on a wound, offering healing where there is hurt, understanding where there is confusion, and reconciliation where there is discord. It's a reminder that in the realm of family, the most potent magik is often found in forgiveness, acceptance, and unconditional love.

Moreover, Frigg's family magik is a testament to the power of protection. It's not just about shielding loved ones from physical harm, but also about safeguarding their emotional and spiritual well-being. Rituals and charms under Frigg's guidance often involve creating protective amulets or talismans, each a symbol of her enduring watchfulness.

As I guide you deeper into the understanding of Frigg's unique family magik, we'll uncover a world where the mundane and the divine intertwine seamlessly. Her teachings show us that the strength of a family lies not just in its unity but in its ability to grow and adapt, to face challenges together, and to find joy in the simple moments of togetherness. I urge you to embrace the nurturing essence of Frigg, to weave her magik into your family life, and to experience the deep, abiding love that is the cornerstone of her legacy.

Family Magik with Frigg

Of all the specialize magik of Norse goddesses, the magik associated with Frigg is mostly concerned with family. Using the ritual below, you can tighten the bonds of a family. By modifying the ritual, you can help a family member who is in crisis, helping them find medical help or financial assistance, heal family rifts, restore contact with a estranged family member. The summoning prayer contains a section where you can modify it, thus the phrase: "Frigg, lend us your strength, let our family ties grow strong and true," can be reworked to say "Frigg, lend us your strength, let our family reunite, bring XX back to us," and so on.

Strengthen Family Ties

Items Needed:

1. Blue or Green Altar Cloth: Representing peace, harmony, and growth within the family.

2. Silver Candles: Symbolizing Frigg's divine energy and the lunar connection to emotions and relationships.

3. Figurine or Image of Frigg: To invoke her presence and assistance in the ritual.

4. Incense (such as Sandalwood or Myrrh): For purifying the space and creating a sacred atmosphere.

5. Clear Quartz Crystals: To amplify intentions and energies.

6. Small Bowls of Water and Salt: Representing purity and the grounding element in family relationships.

7. Family Heirloom or Photographs of Family Members: To symbolize the family and individual members who are the focus of the ritual.

8. Olive Branches or Leaves: Symbolizing peace and reconciliation.

9. Rune Stones (particularly Gebo for gifts and partnerships, and Wunjo for joy and harmony): To incorporate the wisdom of Norse traditions.

Ritual Setup:

- Place the altar cloth on a flat surface.

- Arrange the silver candles and incense in a central position on the altar.

- Set the figurine or image of Frigg as a focal point.

- Place the clear quartz crystals around the figurine or image.

- Position the bowls of water and salt on either side of the altar.

- Lay the family heirloom or photographs around the altar, creating a circle.

- Scatter the olive branches or leaves near the family representations.

- Place the rune stones in front of the figurine or image of Frigg.

Summoning Prayer:

"Frigg, Allmother, nurturer of bonds and guardian of homes,

I call upon your wisdom and your grace.

In your honor, I seek to strengthen the ties that bind my family.

Let understanding and love flow among us, as rivers to the sea.

Guide us to cherish and support each other, in times of joy and strife.

Bless our home with harmony and peace, in every aspect of our life.

Frigg, lend us your strength, let our family ties grow strong and true,

In your compassionate embrace, let our love renew."

Ritual Steps:

1. Light the candles and incense to cleanse the space and welcome Frigg's presence.

2. Hold the quartz crystals and focus on your intention to strengthen family bonds.

3. Place the crystals back on the altar, forming a circle around Frigg's representation.

4. Recite the summoning prayer with sincerity, visualizing your family enveloped in a warm, nurturing light.

5. Sprinkle a pinch of salt into the bowls of water, symbolizing the purification and strengthening of family relationships.

6. Gently touch the family heirloom or photographs, sending your intentions for harmony and unity into each representation.

7. Place the rune stones near the family items, asking for Frigg's blessings of joy, harmony, and partnership.

8. Lay the olive branches or leaves as symbols of peace and reconciliation among family members.

9. Conclude the ritual by expressing gratitude to Frigg for her guidance and blessings.

10. Allow the candles to burn down safely, sealing the intentions set forth in the ritual.

Conclusion:

Keep the family heirloom or photographs in a place of honor, and regularly revisit the altar to reaffirm your intentions. The ritual can be repeated as needed to continuously nurture and strengthen the familial bonds.

Frigg's Love Magik

Positioned prominently within the captivating tapestry that is Norse mythology, Frigg, the revered Allmother, assumes a place of utmost honor, her ethereal essence delicately interlaced with the profound emotions of love and undying loyalty. Her unique love magik is a melody that resonates through the hearts of those who seek it, a harmonious blend of deep affection, understanding, and enduring commitment. In exploring Frigg's love magik, we embark on a journey that reveals the subtle yet profound ways in which love can be nurtured and cherished.

Frigg's love magik is akin to a garden in full bloom, where each flower represents a different aspect of love – trust, respect, passion, and companionship. It is a magik that does not just ignite the flames of new romance but also tends to the embers of long-standing relationships, ensuring that they continue to glow with warmth and light. Her influence in matters of the heart is like the gentle touch of a skilled gardener who knows just how to tend to each plant, ensuring it receives exactly what it needs to thrive.

Central to Frigg's magik is the art of fostering deep emotional connections. It is akin to weaving a beautiful tapestry, where each thread is a shared moment, a whispered secret, or a shared dream. Her rituals and spells focus on enhancing communication and understanding between partners, creating an unbreakable bond that transcends the physical realm. This aspect of her magik is like the roots of an ancient tree, unseen yet vital, providing strength and stability.

In the sphere of romantic love, Frigg's magik shines brightest. She guides lovers in discovering the true essence of their partnership, helping them to see not just with their eyes but with their hearts. Her love spells are not about superficial attraction or fleeting desire; they are about cultivating a love that is deep, genuine, and enduring. It is the kind of love that is patient, kind, and selfless – a love that grows stronger with each passing day.

Frigg's love magik also extends to healing broken hearts and mending strained relationships. It is like the gentle, soothing rain that heals a parched land. Through her guidance, individuals learn to let go of past hurts, to forgive and move forward. Her healing rituals provide comfort and solace, helping individuals to open their hearts to love once again, to trust and to hope.

Furthermore, Frigg's wisdom teaches that true love is not just about taking but also about giving. Her magik encourages selflessness and empathy, reminding us that in loving another, we must also be willing to give of ourselves. It is a love that is generous, understanding, and always ready to offer support and encouragement.

Practicing Frigg's love magik involves simple yet meaningful rituals – lighting a candle to symbolize the enduring flame of love, sharing a meal prepared with intention and care, or exchanging tokens that represent mutual affection and respect. It is about creating moments that celebrate love in all its forms – the quiet, tender moments shared in silence, the joyous laughter that fills a room, the comforting embrace that says more than words ever could.

As this chapter unfolds, the reader is invited to delve into the enchanting world of Frigg's love magik. Each sentence is a step deeper into understanding how to cultivate and cherish love in its purest form. It's an exploration of how to create lasting bonds, heal emotional wounds, and celebrate the joy and beauty of love. Through Frigg's guidance, we learn that love is not just an emotion but a sacred journey, a magikal and transformative experience that enriches our lives in myriad ways.

Frigg Love Magik Ritual

Items Needed:

1. Green or Pink Altar Cloth: Symbolizing love and the nurturing aspect of Frigg.

2. White and Pink Candles: Representing purity of intention and romantic love.

3. Figurine or Image of Frigg: To invoke her presence and blessing.

4. Incense (preferably Rose or Jasmine): For love attraction and to create a harmonious atmosphere.

5. Rose Quartz and Moonstone Crystals: Known for their properties in love and relationships.

6. Bowl of Water with Rose Petals: Symbolizing emotional openness and readiness for love.

7. Paper and Pen: To write down qualities desired in a lover.

8. Honey: To symbolize the sweetness of the desired relationship.

9. Fresh Flowers (especially Roses): As an offering to Frigg, symbolizing love and beauty.

Ritual Setup:

- Lay the altar cloth on a flat surface.

- Arrange the white and pink candles in the center.

- Set the figurine or image of Frigg as a focal point on the altar.

- Place the incense where it can be safely lit.

- Position the rose quartz and moonstone crystals around the figurine or image.

- Prepare the bowl of water with rose petals, placing it on the altar.

- Have the paper, pen, and honey within easy reach.

- Place the fresh flowers near the figurine or image of Frigg as an offering.

Summoning Prayer:

"Frigg, divine weaver of relationships and hearts,

I call upon your gentle guidance in love's art.

Lead me to a lover who's true, kind, and dear,

One who brings joy, and vanquishes fear.

Bless me with love that's pure and right,

Under your watchful gaze, bring this love to light."

Ritual Steps:

1. Light the candles and incense to purify the space and welcome Frigg's presence.

2. Hold the rose quartz and moonstone, focusing on your

desire for a loving, harmonious relationship.

3. Place the crystals back on the altar, encircling Frigg's representation.

4. Recite the summoning prayer with heartfelt intent, envisioning the love you wish to attract.

5. Write down the qualities you seek in a partner on the paper, focusing on emotional and spiritual compatibility.

6. Drizzle a bit of honey over the paper, symbolizing the sweetness and joy of the future relationship.

7. Fold the paper and place it under the figurine or image of Frigg.

8. Gently stir the rose petals in the bowl of water, symbolizing the readiness of your heart for love.

9. Conclude the ritual by expressing gratitude to Frigg for her blessings and guidance.

10. Allow the candles to burn down safely, cementing your intentions in the ritual.

Conclusion:

Keep the rose quartz and moonstone with you as reminders of your intention and to maintain a connection with Frigg's energy in your quest for love. Regularly revisit the altar setup as a reminder of your intent and to reinforce Frigg's presence in your journey to find love.

CHAPTER 8

Seidr and Spae-Craft: The Prophetic Magik of Freya and Frigg

High Magik is commonly associated with the concept of ascension in the realm of magik. When exploring the domain of Norse magik, one cannot overlook the significant role played by Seidr, an ancient art known for its ability to bring about profound transformations and provide remarkable discernment. Seidr, which is often linked with Freya, the Vanadis, is a practice that is veiled in both mystery and power, with its origins tracing back to the core of Norse spiritual traditions. Much like a majestic river that gracefully navigates its way through the diverse landscapes it encounters, this extraordinary form possesses the ability to transform and unravel the concealed intricacies of reality.

Seidr is not mere spellcasting; it is an intricate dance with the energies of the universe. It involves altering the weaves of fate, a practice that demands not only knowledge and skill but also a deep understanding of the interconnectedness of all things. This is the magik of transformation, where you, the practitioner, through rites and rituals, becomes a conduit for divine energies, reshaping reality in accordance with their will and vision.

The process of discernment in Seidr is akin to navigating through a dense forest, where each tree, each leaf, holds a secret waiting to be uncovered. The practitioner learns to attune their senses to the subtle whispers of nature and the hidden messages of the cosmos. Through this heightened awareness, they gain insights into the past, present, and potential futures, their intuition honed to a fine point, like the needle of a compass seeking true north.

However, as with all forms of high magik, Seidr comes with its risks. The very act of tampering with the threads of fate can lead to unintended consequences. A practitioner must approach Seidr with caution and respect, aware that the forces they wield are ancient and powerful, and that their actions can ripple through the fabric of reality in unpredictable ways. The practitioner of Seidr must maintain a balance, ensuring that their actions are in harmony with the greater tapestry of existence.

The practice of Seidr requires a deep connection with the natural world and its cycles. It is a magik that thrives under the open sky, in the quiet of the forest, or by the whispering tides of a moonlit shore. Here, the practitioner can draw upon the elemental energies of the earth, air, fire, and water, weaving them into their rituals and spells.

Rituals in Seidr often involve chanting, drumming, and the use of sacred objects like staves and runes. The chants are ancient verses, powerful and rhythmic, that guide the practitioner into a trance state. In this altered state of consciousness, they journey into the realms beyond the physical, seeking knowledge, power, or healing. This journey is a core aspect of Seidr, a voyage into the unknown that requires courage, focus, and a steadfast heart.

The use of runes in Seidr is particularly significant. These ancient symbols, each a mystery unto itself, are more than mere letters; they are keys to unlocking deeper universal truths. In the hands of a skilled practitioner, runes become tools of divination and transformation, each casting revealing insights into the mysteries of life and the paths laid before the seeker.

In practicing Seidr, one must also be mindful of its connection to the spiritual realm. It is a magik that often involves communication with spirits and deities, a dialogue that requires both reverence and strength of will. The practitioner must learn to navigate these interactions with wisdom, discerning the truths revealed from the illusions that may also present themselves.

Seidr is a world where magik is an intrinsic part of life, where the barriers between different planes of existence are barely discernible, and where the adept can transcend the ordinary and delve into the realm of the divine. This journey is one that entails a profound transformation, guiding individuals towards the revelation of concealed truths and the attainment of complete control over their own fate.

Frigg and spae-craft

The practice of Frigg's spae-craft, deeply intertwined with Norse magik, is renowned for its ability to provide wisdom and insight, making it a beacon of knowledge and foresight. This ancient craft, closely associated with Frigg, the queen of Asgard, is a testament to her profound connection with the threads of fate and destiny. In modern practice, spae-craft finds its place as a powerful tool in divination, offering guidance and perspective to those who seek it.

Frigg's spae-craft is like a compass in the hands of a navigator, traversing the vast ocean of time and possibility. It is an art that requires more than mere intuition; it demands an intimate understanding of the subtle energies that weave the future. In this practice, the diviner becomes a conduit for Frigg's wisdom, channeling her prophetic abilities to gain insights into what may come to pass.

At the heart of Frigg's spae-craft is the practice of rune casting, an ancient method steeped in symbolism and mystery. Each rune, with its complex meanings and associations, is a key to unlocking deeper understandings of the world and the self. In a modern context, rune casting involves meditative focus and a clear intention, as the practitioner seeks guidance or answers from the runes. The runes are cast onto a cloth, each position and combination weaving a narrative that the diviner interprets through the lens of Frigg's wisdom.

Another facet of Frigg's spae-craft is the practice of seer-stones or crystals, used for scrying and seeking visions of potential futures. These stones are not mere tools; they are sacred objects, each infused with the energies of the earth and the divine. In a modern setting, the practitioner gazes into the stone, entering a trance-like state where images, symbols, and scenes may reveal themselves, offering glimpses into possible outcomes and pathways.

Frigg's spae-craft also extends to the reading of natural signs and omens. This practice, akin to reading a book written by the universe itself, involves interpreting the patterns and behaviors of nature, from the flight of birds to the patterns of clouds in the sky. It's an art that requires a deep connection to the natural world and an understanding that everything in existence is interconnected and significant.

The use of animal guides in spae-craft is another powerful element, drawing on the Norse belief in the spiritual significance of animals. These guides, whether encountered in meditative journeys or the natural world, offer wisdom and insight. They serve as messengers from Frigg, each animal embodying different aspects of her knowledge and strength.

In practicing Frigg's spae-craft, one must approach with

respect and openness, understanding that the answers received are not always straightforward. It's a path that requires patience and the willingness to delve into the deeper mysteries of existence. The insights gained through spae-craft are not mere predictions; they are reflections of potential realities, guiding the practitioner towards choices and paths that align with their highest good.

Spae-craft is a practice that offers clarity, guidance, and a deeper understanding of the intricate web of fate that binds us all. Discover how the ancient wisdom of Frigg can be applied in contemporary divination to illuminate the path ahead. Plow ahead, read as much as you can, and create your own interpretation of spae-craft, and use this information as just the starting point.

Practical exercises for enhancing foresight and intuition

Enhancing foresight and intuition is a journey that intertwines the mystic with the pragmatic, leading practitioners to a deeper understanding and connection with the world around them. This journey, rooted in the practice of Norse magik, requires dedication, patience, and a willingness to open oneself to the subtle whispers of the universe.

The first step on this path is the cultivation of mindfulness, a practice that brings one's attention to the present moment in a focused and non-judgmental way. Mindfulness can be honed through simple exercises such as deep, conscious breathing or meditative walks in nature. By attuning oneself to the here and now, the practitioner begins to notice the finer details of their surroundings—the patterns of leaves on a tree, the way shadows play across the ground, the subtle changes in the wind—all of which are integral in developing intuition and foresight.

Rune meditation is another powerful tool. Each rune is not just a symbol but a repository of ancient wisdom. By selecting a rune at random each day and meditating on its meaning and symbolism, practitioners can begin to unlock the deeper insights these symbols hold. This practice requires more than just intellectual understanding; it asks for a deep, intuitive engagement with the rune, allowing its essence to speak to the practitioner in a personal and profound way.

Journaling is an invaluable exercise in this journey. Keeping a record of dreams, feelings, and daily experiences provides a reflective space for insights to emerge. Over time, patterns may become evident—signs and symbols that repeatedly show up, offering guidance or warnings. Journaling fosters a heightened awareness of the subconscious mind, an essential aspect of developing intuition.

Another exercise involves practicing divination, a cornerstone in enhancing foresight. This can begin with simple tarot or oracle card readings, slowly building up to more complex systems like the Norse runes. The key is to approach divination not as a way to see a fixed future, but as a method to understand the potentials and influences at play. It's about learning to ask the right questions and being open to the answers, however unexpected they may be.

Visualization exercises also play a crucial role. These involve picturing scenarios in the mind's eye, focusing on the details and emotions they evoke. Through visualization, practitioners can prepare their minds to recognize and interpret the signs and symbols they may encounter in reality, strengthening their intuitive abilities.

Engaging with nature is a fundamental aspect of enhancing intuition and foresight. The Norse tradition holds a deep reverence for the natural world, seeing it as a source of wisdom and guidance. Regularly spending time in nature, observing its cycles and rhythms, and learning to understand its language can significantly boost one's intuitive abilities. This might involve tracking the phases of the moon, observing the behavior of animals, or simply sitting quietly and listening to the sounds of the earth.

Group work can also be beneficial. Participating in workshops or circles where others share the same journey can provide new perspectives and insights. Group exercises might include shared meditations, rune readings, or discussions on experiences and interpretations. Such interactions can offer validation, encouragement, and different viewpoints, all of which are valuable in developing foresight and intuition.

Lastly, patience and perseverance are key. Developing intuition and foresight is a gradual process; it cannot be rushed. It requires regular practice, an open heart, and a mind willing to listen to the subtle nuances of the universe. The journey is as important as the destination—the insights gained along the way are as valuable as the heightened intuition and foresight that are the ultimate goals.

As you progress through these exercises, you will find your intuitive abilities becoming more acute, their sense of foresight more refined. You will begin to notice signs and omens they may have previously overlooked, understand the deeper meanings behind their dreams, and feel more in tune with the natural world and its messages.

But don't take it too far. Not EVERYTHING you might see contains a special message. Only those things which might cause a fluttering in your solar plexus, or makes you look twice. Then dive into what that might mean.

In this enlightening chapter, we journeyed through the mystical landscapes of Norse magik, delving deep into the profound practices of Seidr and Spae-craft. Our exploration revealed not just the nuances of these ancient arts but also their relevance and application in our modern lives. The key takeaways from this chapter form a tapestry of wisdom, intertwining the old with the new, guiding us towards a more intuitive and magikal understanding of the world.

At the heart of our journey was Seidr, the high magik of transformation and discernment, closely linked with the goddess Freya. This art, rich in its complexity, offers more than mere spell casting; it is an intricate dance with the cosmic energies. Through Seidr, we learned the importance of altering the weaves of fate with care and respect, understanding that each action in this magikal practice can ripple through the fabric of reality. The practitioner of Seidr becomes a weaver of possibilities, navigating through the streams of destiny with a blend of courage and wisdom.

Frigg's Spae-craft, with its profound connection to foresight and divination, offered a complementary perspective. It's a practice that requires not just knowledge but a deep intuitive connection with the natural and spiritual worlds. Through Spae-craft, we learned the art of reading natural signs and omens, interpreting the messages hidden in the mundane, and how this ancient wisdom can be harnessed to illuminate our modern lives.

The practical exercises presented in this chapter are like keys to unlocking our latent potential for intuition and foresight. From mindfulness and rune meditation to journaling and engaging with nature, each exercise serves as a stepping stone towards enhancing our intuitive abilities. These practices encourage us to look within and without, to listen to the whispers of our inner selves, and to observe the language of the universe.

The journey through Seidr and Spae-craft is one of personal transformation. It challenges us to expand our perceptions, to embrace the mysteries of the universe, and to step into a world where magik is as real as the air we breathe. It's a path that requires patience, dedication, and an open heart, but the rewards are immeasurable. As we close this chapter, we are left with a sense of wonder and a deeper connection to the Norse traditions of magik. We carry with us the knowledge that the ancient arts of Seidr and Spae-craft are not relics of the past but vibrant, living practices that can guide us in our quest for wisdom and understanding in the modern world.

Moving on!

CHAPTER 9

The Healing Hands of Frigg: Paths to Wholeness and Health

In the sphere of Norse mythology, where gods and goddesses sway the forces of nature and the fates of mortals, Frigg, the esteemed queen of Asgard, emerges as a beacon of healing and well-being. Her domain, transcending the mere physical, delves into the holistic realms of health, encompassing the mind, body, and spirit. Frigg's healing aspects, rooted in ancient wisdom, offer a path to wholeness that is as relevant today as it was in the days of the Vikings.

Frigg's approach to well-being is like the gentle but persistent rays of the morning sun, slowly warming and revitalizing the earth. She nurtures and heals, not with the immediacy of a sudden storm, but with the steady, pervasive power of a gradually brightening dawn. Her methods are subtle yet profound, working their way into the very fibers of being, mending and fortifying.

Central to Frigg's healing domain is the creation of sacred spaces, environments where balance and harmony preside. These spaces, be they physical locations or spiritual sanctuaries within one's mind, are imbued with energies conducive to healing and rejuvenation. In crafting such spaces, make sure to incorporate elements that resonate with Frigg's essence – soft, nurturing fabrics in calming colors, symbols of her divine aspects like keys or distaffs, and images or statues that represent her nurturing nature.

The crafting of amulets, too, falls within Frigg's purview of healing. These are not mere trinkets, but potent talismans charged with intention and purpose. Creating an amulet under Frigg's guidance involves a ceremonial approach, where each material is chosen for its healing properties and symbolic significance. A practitioner might weave herbs, stones, and symbols into a small pouch, each component a strand in the tapestry of healing magik imbued with Frigg's nurturing energy.

Frigg's wisdom extends into the realm of herbs and natural remedies, her knowledge a treasure trove for those seeking healing through more earthy, tangible means. Her herbal lore is extensive, encompassing plants, roots, and fungi, each with its unique properties and uses. These natural elements are not just ingredients but allies in the healing process, each selected and used with respect and understanding.

Recipes inspired by Frigg's wisdom often involve

combinations of herbs for teas, poultices, or tinctures. These remedies are created not just with an eye for their physical healing properties but also for their energetic qualities. For instance, a tea blend to soothe anxiety might include chamomile for its calming effect, lavender for its stress-relieving properties, and a touch of valerian root, all steeped together in a ritual that invokes Frigg's compassionate energy.

In this exploration of Frigg's healing aspects, we are invited to view well-being through a holistic lens, where the physical, mental, and spiritual elements are intertwined. Her methods teach us that healing is a journey, not a destination – a process of continual nurturing, understanding, and adjustment. As we delve deeper into the wisdom of Frigg, we learn that the paths to health and wholeness are many, each winding and unique, yet all guided by the nurturing hand of the Allmother.

This part of the chapter thus serves as a gateway into the healing arms of Frigg, offering insights and practical knowledge on creating spaces of healing, crafting amulets of protection and well-being, and harnessing the natural world's curative powers. It's an invitation to embrace a more holistic approach to health, inspired by the ancient wisdom of a goddess whose very essence is interwoven with the art of healing.

Creating healing spaces and amulets, inspired by Frigg's gentle wisdom, is an art that transcends mere decoration or craft. These spaces and objects become sanctuaries of rejuvenation and symbols of protection, imbued with energies that resonate with the nurturing essence of Frigg. Each element, carefully chosen and placed, contributes to an atmosphere of harmony and balance, essential for holistic healing.

Imagine stepping into a space dedicated to healing. It's akin to entering a serene forest glade, where the chaos of the outside world fades into a hushed whisper, and a sense of calm pervades the air. This is the essence of a healing space inspired by Frigg. The key lies in creating an environment that feels safe, comforting, and imbued with natural beauty. Soft, flowing fabrics in hues of blue and green might drape the walls, reminiscent of the sky and the earth, elements deeply connected to Frigg. Gentle lighting, perhaps the flicker of candles or the soft glow of lamps, casts the room in a soothing ambiance, while a gentle fragrance of lavender and chamomile fills the air, calming the senses and inviting relaxation.

In the center of this space, a small altar can be set up, a focal point for healing energies. On this altar, symbols of Frigg can be placed – a spindle or distaff, representing her connection to domesticity and creation, or a small figure of a mother cradling a child, symbolizing her role as a nurturer. Fresh flowers, crystals like moonstone or rose quartz, and a bowl of water can also be added, each element bringing its unique energy to the space.

The creation of healing amulets is another significant

aspect of working with Frigg's energies. These amulets are more than just jewelry; they are talismans, charged with intentions of health, well-being, and protection. Crafting an amulet might begin with selecting a piece of cloth in soothing colors, into which herbs associated with healing – such as lavender for relaxation, sage for cleansing, or thyme for strength – are placed. Small stones or crystals can also be added, each chosen for their healing properties. The cloth can then be tied with a ribbon or string, while the practitioner chants or silently focuses on their intention for the amulet. This process is not just about the physical creation but also about pouring one's energy and focus into the amulet, charging it with healing power.

In addition to these physical elements, the energy of the space and the amulet is further enhanced through ritual. This might involve burning incense, playing soft, rhythmic music, or reciting healing prayers or poems. The idea is to engage all senses, creating a holistic healing experience. The practitioner, in tuning into Frigg's energy, acts as a conduit, channeling her nurturing and restorative powers into the space and the amulet.

As one engages in these practices, the healing space and the amulets become infused with the essence of Frigg, each becoming a sanctuary and a source of comfort and strength. Through these techniques, we not only honor the ancient wisdom of Frigg but also bring her healing energies into our lives in a tangible, meaningful way. This part of the chapter thus serves as a guide, rich in detail and insight, on how to create spaces and objects that resonate with the healing power of the Norse goddess, transforming ordinary environments and items into sacred tools of healing and protection.

High Magik Ritual to Activate and Charge an Amulet or Sanctify a Healing Space Dedicated to Frigg

Items Needed:

1. Altar Cloth: Preferably in blue or green, symbolizing tranquility and healing.

2. White Candles: For purity and to invite positive energy.

3. Incense: Lavender or sage, for calming and cleansing properties.

4. Crystals: Moonstone or rose quartz, known for their healing energies.

5. Small Bowl of Water: Representing emotional clarity and purity.

6. Herbs: Such as lavender, sage, and thyme, tied in a small bundle.

7. Amulet or Symbolic Object: To be charged or a representation of the healing space.

8. Rune Stones: For divination and to connect with Norse traditions.

9. Offering Bowl: For offerings to Frigg.

Ritual Setup:

- Lay the altar cloth on a flat surface.

- Place the white candles in the center of the altar.

- Arrange the incense so that it can safely burn, filling the space with its fragrance.

- Position the crystals and the bowl of water on the altar.

- Place the bundle of herbs beside the bowl.

- Set the amulet or representation of the healing space on the altar.

- Have the rune stones and offering bowl within easy reach.

Summoning Prayer:

"Great Frigg, Allmother, keeper of wisdom and healing,
I call upon your grace and nurturing spirit.
Bless this space (or this amulet) with your divine light,
Infuse it with your profound insight and protection.
As the moon governs the tides, govern the energies here,
Let them flow with healing, purity, and peace.
I offer these symbols in your honor,
May they resonate with your strength and care.
Guide my hands and heart in this sacred act,
Frigg, bless this space (or amulet) with your sacred pact."

Ritual Steps:

1. Light the candles and the incense to purify the space and invite Frigg's presence.

2. Hold the amulet (or focus on the symbolic representation of the space) in your hands, closing your eyes, and recite the summoning prayer with sincere intention.

3. Pass the amulet (or move your hands over the symbolic representation of the space) through the incense smoke gently, visualizing it being cleansed and blessed.

4. Sprinkle a few drops of water from the bowl onto the amulet (or in the space) while envisioning it being imbued with clarity and emotional healing.

5. Place the amulet back on the altar and surround it with the crystals and herb bundle, focusing on channeling healing and protective energies into it.

6. Pick up each rune stone, asking for guidance and insight as you charge the amulet, or sanctify the space.

7. Place offerings in the offering bowl as a gesture of gratitude to Frigg.

8. Close the ritual by giving thanks to Frigg for her blessings and extinguish the candles.

After the ritual, the amulet is ready to wear or keep in a sacred space, and the area designated for healing is consecrated, both carrying the blessings and protection of Frigg.

Herbal Knowledge with Frigg

In the verdant realm of Norse magik, the herbal wisdom of Frigg, the revered Allmother, stands as a testament to the healing power of nature. Drawing from Frigg's profound knowledge, we uncover an array of herbs, each with its unique properties and uses, woven into recipes that are as nurturing as they are potent. This exploration into herbal lore is not just a journey through traditional remedies but a path to deeper understanding and connection with the natural world.

Frigg, known for her nurturing and protective qualities, is closely associated with herbs that offer healing and comfort. Among these is the humble yet powerful chamomile, a herb revered for its calming properties. Chamomile, with its delicate, daisy-like flowers, is a symbol of peace and tranquility. A simple chamomile tea, steeped in boiling water and perhaps sweetened with a touch of honey, can be a soothing remedy for anxiety and stress, embodying Frigg's nurturing spirit.

Another herb in Frigg's arsenal is lavender, known for its lovely scent and its ability to soothe both the mind and body. Lavender can be used in various ways – as an essential oil for relaxation, dried in sachets to promote peaceful sleep, or infused in bathwater for a calming soak. These lavender-based remedies are not just about physical well-being; they are about creating a space of serenity and balance, much like Frigg's own abode, Fensalir.

Sage, a herb with deep cleansing and protective qualities, is also under Frigg's domain. Burning sage as a smudging ritual can purify a space, clearing it of negative energy and inviting in protection and wisdom. This practice, rooted in ancient traditions, resonates with Frigg's role as a guardian and guide, her essence safeguarding and enlightening those who seek her aid.

Frigg's wisdom also extends to the art of concocting healing salves and balms. A simple recipe might involve blending beeswax with infused oils – such as calendula for its skin-healing properties, or St. John's wort for its anti-inflammatory effects – creating a balm that soothes and repairs. These salves, crafted with intent and care, are imbued with the healing energy of the herbs and the nurturing power of Frigg.

The Allmother's herbal knowledge encompasses not just physical healing but emotional and spiritual well-being. A tea blend inspired by her wisdom might include rose petals for emotional upliftment, lemon balm for its mood-enhancing properties, and a hint of mint for clarity and focus. This blend, steeped in hot water and enjoyed in a moment of quiet reflection, can be a balm for the soul, a drink that calms the mind and uplifts the spirit.

In crafting these herbal remedies and recipes, it is essential to approach them with respect for the plants and their energies. Each herb, each ingredient, is a gift from nature, a piece of the earth's abundance. The act of creating these remedies is in itself a ritual, a sacred process that honors the connection between the human and the natural world.

In this captivating chapter, we delved into the verdant world of Frigg, the Allmother, exploring her profound influence over well-being and her mastery of healing arts. The key takeaways from this chapter form a mosaic of ancient wisdom and practical knowledge, offering a pathway to holistic health and spiritual wholeness, deeply rooted in the traditions of Norse magik.

We began our journey by exploring Frigg's domain over well-being, where her nurturing essence envelops the realm of healing. Here, we learned that health is not just a physical state but a harmonious balance of mind, body, and spirit. Frigg, with her deep connection to the natural world, emerges as a guiding force, her wisdom echoing through the ages as a beacon of comfort and healing. Her approach to well-being, akin to the gentle nurturing of the earth itself, reminds us of the importance of harmony and balance in our pursuit of health.

The creation of healing spaces and amulets, inspired by Frigg's gentle touch, stood as a testament to the power of intention and environment in the healing process. We discovered techniques to infuse our surroundings and objects with healing energies, turning them into sanctuaries of rejuvenation and symbols of protection. These practices are not mere rituals; they are transformative acts that invite Frigg's nurturing energy into our lives, creating spaces and talismans that resonate with her essence.

Moreover, we ventured into the realm of herbal knowledge, where Frigg's wisdom shines brightly. Her connection to herbs like chamomile, lavender, and sage opened doors to a world where each plant holds a key to healing. We learned how these herbs could be used to create teas, salves, and balms, each recipe a blend of practical healing and ancient magik. These herbal remedies, crafted with care and respect for nature's gifts, are not just about treating ailments but about fostering a deeper connection with the natural world and the nurturing spirit of Frigg.

In summing up this chapter, we are left with a treasure trove of knowledge and insights into Frigg's healing powers. From creating spaces of harmony to crafting amulets of protection, from delving into the rich world of herbal lore to imbibing the essence of each plant, we have journeyed through practices that invite health, balance, and well-being into our lives. This chapter is more than just a reading; it's an invitation to embrace Frigg's healing hands, to integrate her wisdom into our daily practices, and to walk a path that leads to wholeness and health, guided by the nurturing spirit of the Allmother.

CHAPTER 10

The Abundance of Freya: Magik for Wealth and Prosperity

In the enchanting realm of Norse magik, where the old gods still whisper their secrets to those who listen, Freya, the goddess of love and war, also emerges as a beacon of abundance and prosperity. Her energy, as vibrant and life-giving as the golden fields of summer, is a powerful ally in rituals and spells designed to attract wealth and abundance. This part of the chapter invites us into the world of Freya's abundance magik, revealing how her energy can be harnessed to enrich our lives.

Imagine Freya's energy as a golden river, flowing with the promise of prosperity and success. In rituals to attract abundance, this river becomes a source from which practitioners can draw. The first step in such rituals often involves setting up a sacred space – an altar adorned with symbols of Freya, like golden or green cloth representing her vitality and wealth, and a figurine or image of the goddess herself. Candles, preferably in gold, silver, or green, are lit to evoke the energy of wealth, while the air is filled with the scent of cinnamon or mint incense, known for their associations with money and prosperity.

The heart of these rituals lies in the invocation of Freya, where practitioners, with respect and clarity of purpose, call upon her to bless their endeavors. They might chant or sing, their voices weaving through the candlelight, asking for Freya's aid in unlocking doors of opportunity and abundance. This invocation is not just a plea, but an alignment of the practitioner's energy with Freya's boundless vitality.

To further draw upon Freya's energy, practitioners often engage in the magikal act of visualization. They might close their eyes and envision themselves surrounded by the abundance they seek, whether it's a flow of financial wealth, success in business ventures, or fruitful personal projects. This visualization is imbued with the energy of Freya, transforming it from a mere daydream into a powerful magikal working.

An important aspect of these rituals is the offering – giving something back to honor Freya's generosity. This might be a libation of mead or honey, or even a piece of amber or gold. These offerings are made with gratitude, acknowledging the reciprocal nature of the relationship between the practitioner and the divine.

As the ritual concludes, practitioners often carry a piece of the ritual with them – it could be a stone charged during the ritual, a written affirmation of their intent, or a small token representing Freya's abundance. This object serves as a talisman, a constant reminder of the abundance that is flowing towards them.

In Freya's connection to fertility, not just in the physical sense but also in the growth of personal endeavors, lies the next phase of our exploration. Just as she nurtures the growth of crops and the passion within hearts, she also fosters the growth of dreams and aspirations. Here, we delve deeper into how Freya's energy can be channeled to bring forth prosperity in various facets of life, exploring how her fertile and generous essence can be a catalyst for personal growth and success.

Freya's connection to fertility and growth in personal endeavors

In the mystical narrative of Norse mythology, Freya's essence extends far beyond the realms of love and beauty, deeply intertwining with the concepts of fertility and growth. Her connection to these forces is not just about the fertility of the earth or the procreation of beings; it's an allegorical representation of the flourishing of personal endeavors and aspirations. This part of the chapter unveils how Freya's fertile energy can be harnessed to nurture and expand one's personal goals and projects.

Visualize Freya's energy as the first rays of dawn that

touch the earth, awakening the sleeping seeds beneath the soil, stirring them to life. Similarly, her energy acts upon personal projects and ambitions, awakening them, infusing them with vitality and the promise of growth. She is like the gardener who knows exactly what each plant needs to bloom; under her guidance, ideas and dreams are nurtured to their fullest potential.

Engaging with Freya for personal growth involves recognizing and tapping into the cycles of nature, mirroring the ebb and flow of energies in one's own life. Just as the seasons cycle from spring to winter, personal endeavors too have their seasons of planting, growing, harvesting, and resting. Freya's connection to these natural rhythms provides a template for managing and advancing one's goals. By aligning one's actions with these cycles, efforts become more harmonious and effective, resonating with the natural order of things.

Incorporating Freya's energy into personal endeavors often begins with a ritual or a symbolic act. This could be planting a physical seed while setting an intention for a project, or creating a vision board that captures the essence of one's aspirations. These acts are symbolic of planting the seeds of one's ambitions in the fertile ground of Freya's energy, entrusting them to her nurturing powers.

Moreover, Freya's association with cats – creatures known for their independence and resilience – serves as a metaphor for the journey of personal growth. Like cats, one must approach their goals with determination and flexibility, balancing independence with the need for nurturing and support. Invoking Freya in this context means seeking the balance between self-reliance and the need for divine guidance and assistance.

Fertility in Freya's domain also symbolizes the concept of abundance and prosperity – not just in material terms but in richness of experience and personal fulfillment. To draw upon this aspect of her energy, practitioners might engage in affirmations or visualization exercises, picturing their endeavors not only succeeding but also enriching their life with abundance and joy.

As we further explore Freya's influence in personal growth, we begin to understand that fertility and growth are not merely about external achievements but also about inner development and enrichment. Freya's role transcends the physical, touching the spiritual, emotional, and intellectual facets of one's being. Her guidance aids in cultivating qualities like creativity, resilience, and wisdom, which are crucial for personal growth.

In the next segment, the focus shifts to the art of crafting talismans under Freya's guidance. These talismans serve as physical representations of Freya's nurturing energy, imbued with the intention of bringing forth prosperity and success. They are not just mere objects but potent symbols that carry the vibrancy of Freya's fertile essence, aiding the practitioner in their journey towards achieving their goals and realizing their dreams.

Crafting Freya's Magikal Talismans

Within the complex realm of Norse magic, the act of fashioning talismans while under the wise and insightful guidance of Freya can be likened to the meticulous art of weaving an individualized charm that is infused with the powerful energies of prosperity and success bestowed by the goddess herself. With her dual role as the deity of love and war, Freya also holds dominion over abundance, thus making her the ideal divine archetype for individuals who aspire to manifest wealth and prosperity. The crafting of these talismans is not just a simple artistic endeavor, but rather a complex and intricate process.

The process begins with selecting the right materials, which act as conduits for Freya's energy. A common choice is green or gold fabric or leather, symbolizing growth and wealth. This material forms the base of the talisman. It can be shaped into a small bag or pouch, or a more intricate design, depending on the practitioner's skill and preference. The color choice is essential, as it sets the intention of the talisman, aligning it with the energies of growth and abundance.

Next, symbols representing Freya and her aspects of fertility and prosperity are chosen. These might include images of a cat, her sacred animal; a representation of Brisingamen, her famed necklace; or runes such as Fehu (wealth), Berkano (new beginnings, growth), and Jera (harvest, reward). These symbols can be drawn, embroidered, or carved onto the talisman, each stroke a meditation on the qualities they represent and an invocation of Freya's presence and power.

Crystals play a significant role in charging the talisman with Freya's energy. Stones such as citrine, known for attracting wealth, or green aventurine, associated with prosperity and good fortune, are excellent choices. These crystals can be placed within the talisman or attached to it, their natural energies harmonizing with the intention of attracting abundance.

Herbs are another crucial element. Basil, known for attracting wealth, and cinnamon, associated with success and power, are often included. These herbs can be dried and placed within the talisman, lending their energies to its purpose. As they are added, the practitioner focuses on their intention, infusing the herbs with their desire for prosperity and success.

As the talisman is assembled, a ritual to consecrate and charge it is performed. This ritual might involve laying the talisman on an altar dedicated to Freya, surrounded by candles in green or gold, and incense such as patchouli or sandalwood. The practitioner then calls upon Freya, asking her to bless the talisman with her energies of abundance and growth. A prayer or chant can be recited, such as:

"Freya, Goddess of abundance, love, and might,

Bless this talisman in your sacred light.

Bring prosperity, success, and wealth my way,

As I honor you on this day."

The ritual concludes with the practitioner wearing or carrying the talisman or placing it in a location where it can attract the desired abundance. It's essential to remember that the talisman is a magikal tool, a focus for the practitioner's intentions and desires, amplified by Freya's potent energies.

In creating a talisman under Freya's guidance, the practitioner embarks on a journey of personal growth and empowerment. They align their energy with the divine, tapping into the abundant flow of the universe. The talisman becomes a symbol of this alignment, a physical manifestation of their desire for prosperity and the blessings of Freya. This part of the chapter not only provides a detailed guide to crafting such a talisman but also invites the reader into a deeper understanding of Freya's role in Norse magik and the power of personal intention in creating a life of abundance and success.

Wealth Ritual to Freya

At first glance, this may seem like a generic ritual to Freya, but it's quite powerful. In testing (and I love testing!) I had no idea how fast Freya might work. My daughter needed some assistance, and I was somewhat empty in my bank accounts, so after testing this ritual, using a specific request:

"Quick and easy cash injection into my bank accounts" I woke the next morning to not one, but TWO one-on-one mentoring clients. Yes, and due to daily deposits from the payment service, that money was also waiting the very next day.

Let's get started, shall we? (* I was going to say "no further ado... etc." But I detest that phrase now, having heard it way too much in many video tutorials on a popular video streaming service.)

This ritual calls upon the abundant energies of Freya, Norse goddess of love, beauty, and fertility, to attract wealth and prosperity. It combines elements symbolizing wealth and Freya's divine essence, creating a magikal space for manifesting financial abundance.

Materials Needed:

Green or Gold Cloth (Altar Cover): Symbolizes growth and wealth.

Gold or Green Candles: Represents prosperity and Freya's energy.

Small Figurine or Picture of Freya, Freya's Sigil (back of book) - To focus the invocation on Freya.

Bowl of Soil: Symbolizes fertility and grounding.

Incense (Preferably Jasmine or Sandalwood): For purification and to please Freya.

Crystals such as Citrine or Pyrite: Known for attracting

wealth.

Pen and Paper: To write down your intentions regarding wealth.

Offerings for Freya: Such as honey, mead, or fresh fruits.

A Small Bowl of Water: Represents flow and emotional clarity.

Ritual Steps:

Prepare the Altar: Cover a flat surface with green or gold cloth. Arrange the gold or green candles in the center, place the figurine or picture of Freya prominently, and set the bowl of soil and crystals on the altar.

Cleanse the Space: Light the incense to purify the space. Let its aroma fill the area, creating a sacred and welcoming atmosphere for Freya.

Set Your Intentions: Write down your specific goals related to wealth and prosperity on the paper. Be as clear and detailed as possible. See my example above.

Invoke Freya: Light the candles and focus on the image or figurine of Freya. Recite the invocation prayer:

"Freya, goddess of abundance and grace,

I call upon your radiant face.

Bless my path with prosperity,

Let wealth flow endlessly to me.

With heart open and spirit bright,

Guide me under your nurturing light."

Offerings: Place your offerings before the image of Freya. Pour the honey or mead over the fruits or place them neatly in a bowl as a symbol of gratitude and reverence.

Charge the Crystals to create a Talisman: Hold the crystals in your hands and visualize your intentions flowing into them. Imagine a golden light of abundance enveloping the stones.

Seal the Intentions: Place the crystals back on the altar and the written intentions in the bowl of soil, symbolizing the planting of seeds for future prosperity.

Water Offering: Gently pour the water over the soil and paper, visualizing your intentions growing and flourishing.

Closing the Ritual: Thank Freya for her presence and blessings. Blow out the candles or let them burn down safely.

After the Ritual: Keep the charged crystals with you as a reminder of your intentions. Regularly revisit your intentions written on the paper, reinforcing your connection to Freya and your goals.

This ritual is a blend of intention setting, divine invocation, and symbolic actions, all aimed at aligning oneself with the energies of abundance and the powerful guidance of

Freya. The simplicity of the offerings and steps ensures that anyone, regardless of their path or experience, can perform this ritual and tap into the prosperous energies Freya offers.

CHAPTER 11

The Shield of the Vanir: Protective Magik with Freya

In the rich and varied tapestry of Norse mythology, Freya, often revered for her beauty and love, also embodies the formidable strength of a warrior. This aspect of Freya, her warrior spirit, offers a profound source of inspiration for protective workings in magik. Understanding Freya's role as a warrior is to tap into a reservoir of strength and courage, essential for crafting effective protective wards and spells.

Freya's warrior aspect is like the fierce and majestic falcon, her chosen avatar, surveying the landscape with keen eyes, ready to swoop down and shield those under her watch. She is not only a nurturer but also a protector, her prowess in battle as celebrated as her powers of love and fertility. To invoke Freya's warrior energy in protective magik is to call upon her indomitable spirit, her fearless nature, and her strategic mind.

One of the most striking images of Freya in her warrior

aspect is her role as the leader of the Valkyries, the choosers of the slain. In this role, she rides into battle, not for conquest or glory, but as a guardian, a protector of the worthy. Her presence on the battlefield is both a blessing and a shield, her selection of fallen warriors a testament to her discernment and respect for bravery and honor. This image serves as a powerful symbol for protective workings, where you seek not just to ward off harm but to embody the qualities of vigilance, discernment, and strength.

Incorporating Freya's warrior energy into protective magik begins with setting an intention that resonates with her attributes. It involves recognizing one's inner strength and the power to overcome challenges. Practitioners might create a ritual space that honors Freya's warrior aspect, perhaps adorning it with symbols of falcons or swords, or images depicting her as a battle-ready goddess. This space becomes a sacred ground, a fortress of spiritual strength where protective energies are conjured and honed.

The actual crafting of wards and spells under Freya's guidance often involves invoking her through chants or prayers that emphasize her protective nature. For instance, a practitioner might recite:

"Freya, mighty warrior, shield and guide,
In your strength, I take pride.

Around me, cast your protective ring,

Under your watchful eye, I am under no being's wing."

As these words are spoken, you visualize a protective barrier forming around them, imbued with Freya's strength and resilience. This barrier is not just a physical shield but also a spiritual one, guarding against negative energies, ill will, or any form of harm.

Moreover, working with Freya's warrior aspect is also about empowerment, about awakening one's own martial spirit. It's a journey of discovering personal power and the capacity to stand strong in the face of adversity. Through Freya's example, practitioners learn to harness their inner warrior, to confront fears, and to assert their right to be safe and protected.

As we transition from understanding Freya's warrior aspect to the practical application of this knowledge in crafting protective wards and spells, we carry with us the image of Freya as a fierce protector. Her energy not only fortifies our magikal workings but also empowers us to be active participants in our own safeguarding. Freya's warrior spirit is a reminder that sometimes, the best protection lies in embracing our own strength and resolve.

In the mystical tradition of Norse magik, where ancient lore and modern practice intertwine, crafting protective wards and spells for personal safeguarding stands as a fundamental aspect of one's spiritual defense. Drawing upon Freya's warrior aspect, these protective workings are not just about creating barriers against harm but also about empowering oneself with her strength and foresight. Let's examine the practical aspects of constructing such wards and spells, a process akin to building an invisible fortress fortified by the energies of the divine.

Imagine crafting a protective ward as laying the foundation of a magikal fortress. The first step involves selecting the right location – a space where you feel safe and at peace, be it a corner of your room, a personal altar, or even a space in your mind. Here, the wards will be established, creating a sanctuary shielded from negative influences. Just as a fortress is built on solid ground, so too must your wards be grounded in clear intention and purpose.

The selection of materials and symbols for your wards is crucial. Common items like crystals, particularly black tourmaline, or obsidian, known for their protective properties, can serve as the cornerstone of your wards. These stones can be charged under the light of the moon, a celestial body closely associated with Freya, to infuse them with her energy. Alongside, symbols of Freya, such as images of falcons or representations of her chariot pulled by cats, can be placed within the space, serving as a constant reminder of her protective presence.

The actual crafting of the ward involves a ritualistic

process, where each item is placed with intention. As you lay each stone or symbol, visualize a shield of light emanating from them, encircling the space in a protective embrace. Chanting or softly singing a prayer to Freya can enhance this visualization, weaving your voice into the fabric of the ward:

"Freya, guardian fierce and bold,

In your strength, let my protection unfold.

Around this space, a shield of light,

Guarded by your warrior might."

This incantation serves as a beacon, calling upon Freya's energy to fortify your wards. The act of chanting not only imbues the space with protective energy but also aligns your spirit with Freya's resilience, turning the ward into a dynamic, living extension of her power.

In addition to physical wards, crafting personal spells for safeguarding is equally important. These spells often involve a combination of spoken words, herbs, and personal symbols. For instance, a simple protection spell might involve writing a statement of intent on a piece of parchment, anointing it with protective oils like frankincense or myrrh, and then burning it to release its energies. As the smoke rises, it carries your intentions to Freya, asking for her shield to surround you.

As the chapter progresses, the narrative seamlessly

transitions from the construction of protective wards to the empowerment that comes from tapping into Freya's martial spirit. This shift underscores the holistic nature of protection in Norse magik - it's not just about warding off external threats but also about internal strengthening. Under Freya's guidance, the practitioner learns that true safeguarding encompasses both the physical and the spiritual realms, and that the greatest shield one can wield is the power of their own spirit, honed and fortified by the divine energies of the gods.

Embracing the martial spirit of Freya in the practice of magik is not merely about invoking the attributes of a warrior; it is a profound journey of self-empowerment. This facet of Freya, often overshadowed by her roles in love and beauty, is a powerful aspect that speaks of strength, resilience, and strategic acumen. It is in understanding and harnessing this martial spirit that practitioners can find empowerment in their magikal practices and personal lives.

The martial spirit of Freya stands as a testament to the duality of existence – the ability to harbor both nurturing love and fierce protectiveness. It's a reminder that strength does not negate gentleness, and power can coexist with compassion. In the Norse tradition, Freya, as a leader of the Valkyries, embodies this duality. She rides into battle, not as a figure of terror, but as a symbol of honor and valor, choosing those who have fallen bravely. To tap into this energy is to awaken one's own inner warrior, the part of oneself that is unyielding, fearless, and strategic in the face of life's battles.

Empowerment through Freya's martial spirit begins with self-awareness. It's about recognizing your own inner strength and the reservoirs of power that lie within. It involves developing a mindset that is both resilient and adaptable, capable of facing challenges head-on while also being compassionate and mindful. This is the essence of Freya's warrior aspect – the ability to be formidable in protection and defense, yet also caring and wise.

Incorporating this spirit into magik involves rituals and spells that focus on personal empowerment. These might include meditations where one visualizes themselves embodying the qualities of Freya as a warrior. It could be as simple as standing tall, imagining oneself clad in armor, imbued with Freya's strength and courage. This visualization is not about preparing for physical battle but about fortifying the spirit, readying oneself for the challenges of life.

Another aspect of this empowerment is developing strategic thinking. Freya, in her warrior aspect, is not only strong but also wise and tactful. Practitioners can draw upon this by approaching their problems and obstacles with a combination of intuition and calculated strategy. It's about planning your moves, anticipating outcomes, and being prepared to face any situation with confidence and intelligence.

Rituals invoking Freya's martial spirit can also include

crafting amulets or talismans that represent her warrior aspect. Items such as a pendant shaped like a sword or a shield, charged with the intention of empowerment and protection, serve as constant reminders of the practitioner's own strength and resilience. These objects, when worn or carried, act as conduits of Freya's energy, providing a sense of empowerment and security.

Chanting or reciting affirmations dedicated to Freya can also reinforce this sense of empowerment. Phrases like "I embody the strength and wisdom of Freya" or "With Freya's might, I face my challenges" can be powerful tools in building self-confidence and inner strength.

In summary, embracing the martial spirit of Freya is about more than just seeking protection; it's a path to personal empowerment. It's about finding the warrior within, a being of strength, honor, and wisdom. As we conclude this part of the chapter, the narrative gracefully transitions from understanding Freya's warrior aspect to practical applications in rituals and daily life, leaving the reader with a sense of being emboldened and inspired, ready to harness their inner strength in the pursuit of their magikal and mundane goals.

Ritual for Protection of Self or Family Using Freya's Energy

The purpose of this ritual is to tap into the powerful and defensive energy of Freya in order to ensure the safety and protection of oneself or one's family. By combining various elements that symbolize strength, vigilance, and the nurturing protection of Freya, a powerful magikal shield is formed around the practitioner or their loved ones.

Materials Needed:

Red or Gold Altar Cloth: Represents Freya's warrior strength and divine energy.

White Candles: Symbolize purity, protection, and clarity.

Image or Symbol of Freya: To focus the invocation and channel her energy.

Incense (preferably Cedar or Sage): Used for cleansing and protective purposes.

Small Bowl of Salt: Represents grounding and protection.

Crystals like Black Tourmaline or Amethyst: Known for their protective properties.

A Small Container of Water: Symbolizes emotional clarity and cleansing.

Offerings for Freya: Such as honey, wine, or bread.

Personal Items or Photographs of Family Members: To direct the protective energy specifically.

Ritual Steps:

Prepare the Space: Cover the altar with the red or gold cloth. Arrange the white candles around the image or symbol of

Freya. Place the bowl of salt, the water container, and the crystals on the altar.

Cleansing the Space: Light the incense, allowing its smoke to purify the area. Move around the space with the incense, visualizing it clearing away negative energies.

Setting Intention: Hold the crystals in your hand and focus on your intention for protection. Visualize a protective shield enveloping you or your family.

Invocation of Freya: Light the candles and focus on the image or symbol of Freya. Recite the invocation prayer:

"Freya, mighty goddess of protection and strength,
I call upon your power at length.
Shield me (or my family) with your warrior light,
Keep us safe, both day and night."

Offerings: Place your offerings before the image of Freya. Pour the wine or drizzle the honey over the bread as a gesture of gratitude and respect.

Activating the Salt and Water: Sprinkle the salt into the water while continuing to focus on your protective intention. The salt-infused water now acts as a purifying and protective agent.

Anointing: Dip your fingers in the saltwater and anoint the personal items or photographs, as well as the doorways and windows of your home. As you do this, imagine each anointing reinforcing the protective barrier.

Closing the Ritual: Thank Freya for her guidance and protection. Extinguish the candles or allow them to burn down safely.

After the Ritual: Dispose of the offerings in a respectful manner, either by burying, leaving them in nature, or consuming them if appropriate. Keep the crystals with you or in a common area of your home to maintain the protective energy.

This ritual is a powerful way to invoke Freya's protective energy, creating a magikal barrier against harm while also nurturing the practitioner's or family's emotional and spiritual well-being. It's a holistic approach to protection, channeling the strength and vigilance of one of Norse mythology's most revered deities.

CHAPTER 12

Lesser known Aspects of Freya and Frigg's magik

In the vast and intricate world of Norse magik, the familiar tales of Freya and Frigg's powers in love, beauty, and protection only scratch the surface of their divine capabilities. Beneath the well-trodden paths of their more renowned magikal practices lie lesser known, yet equally potent, aspects of their sorcery. This part of the chapter draws back the veil on these hidden facets, revealing a deeper, more nuanced understanding of both goddesses' magikal influence.

The first of these lesser-known aspects is their connection to seiðr, an ancient form of Norse magik often associated with prophecy and altering fate. While Freya is traditionally seen as a deity of love and fertility, she is also a master of seiðr, teaching this art to the gods themselves. Her mastery of seiðr is a powerful reminder of her deep understanding of the mystical forces that weave the tapestry of existence. In exploring this aspect of

Freya's power, practitioners can tap into her profound knowledge of fate and destiny, learning to weave their own paths through the complex patterns of life.

Frigg, too, holds her own secrets in the realm of magik. Often depicted as a nurturing mother and devoted wife, she possesses a deep connection to the wisdom of the natural world and the mysteries of the divine. Her ability to see into the future, though she never reveals what she knows, is a testament to her deep understanding of the inevitable flow of events. This aspect of Frigg's power speaks to her ability to guide and protect, offering silent, knowing support as the fates unfold.

Another lesser-explored aspect of Freya and Frigg's magik lies in their influence over dreams and the subconscious. In Norse lore, dreams were not mere figments of the imagination but messages from the divine, pathways to hidden truths and insights. Freya, with her connection to the mystical and the sensual, can guide practitioners in interpreting these dream messages, revealing paths to self-discovery and enlightenment. Similarly, Frigg's maternal intuition and foresight make her a guardian of dreams, offering protection and wisdom as one navigates the shadowy realms of the subconscious.

Next up, the use of runes in Norse magikal practices. Runes, the ancient alphabet used by the Norse, are more than just letters – they are symbols of cosmic powers and deep mysteries. Working with runes under the guidance of Freya and Frigg can unlock potent energies for divination, spellwork, and self-discovery. Each rune is a key to understanding the forces that shape the world and our destinies within it. As practitioners learn to interpret and harness the power of these runes, they open themselves to a deeper understanding of the universe and their place within it, guided by the wisdom and power of Freya and Frigg.

Working with dreams and the subconscious.

In the labyrinthine world of Norse magik, the exploration of dreams and the subconscious stands as a journey into a realm as mysterious and deep as the night sky. This exploration, akin to navigating the shadowy realms of the mind, is a venture where one uncovers hidden truths and gains profound insights. Here, in the realm of dreams and the subconscious, practitioners can connect with the underlying currents of their psyche, tapping into the wisdom that lies beneath the conscious mind.

Consider dreams as the whispering winds of the subconscious, carrying messages from the deepest parts of our psyche. These nightly visions are more than mere figments of imagination; they are a tapestry woven with the threads of our deepest fears, hopes, and desires. In Norse magik, working with dreams is akin to deciphering an ancient and sacred language, where each symbol and scenario holds a key to understanding our innermost selves. This practice is not just about interpreting dreams; it's about engaging with them, learning to listen and communicate with the subconscious mind.

The process begins with cultivating a mindful approach to dreams. Just as a gardener tenderly cares for their plants, so must the practitioner nurture their relationship with their dreams. This can start with simple steps like keeping a dream journal, recording each dream with as much detail as possible upon waking. This act of recording is not merely for remembrance; it is an act of reverence, acknowledging the importance and value of these nocturnal messages.

Engaging with dreams under the guidance of Freya and Frigg involves more than passive observation. It requires an active engagement, where the practitioner learns to enter a dream with intention. This can be achieved through techniques like lucid dreaming, where one becomes conscious within a dream and can interact with it knowingly. Imagine standing in a dream, aware that you are dreaming, and able to converse with the characters and symbols around you. This is the essence of working with dreams in Norse magik – an active dialogue with the subconscious.

The dreamscape is a fertile ground for magikal work. Here, in this ethereal realm, practitioners can perform rituals, seek guidance, and even heal emotional wounds. By visualizing a sacred space within the dream, they can create a sanctuary where they can safely explore their inner world. This space can be a reflection of their physical altar or a completely new creation, tailored to the needs of their subconscious mind.

As the chapter progresses, the narrative delves into practical techniques for dream work, such as meditation before sleep to set intentions, using specific herbs or crystals that enhance dreaming, or practicing guided visualizations that help in traversing the dreamscape. These techniques are not just tools; they are bridges between the conscious and the subconscious, allowing a flow of communication and understanding.

Embarking on the mystical journey of dreamwork under the auspices of Freya and Frigg offers a gateway to the subconscious, revealing hidden truths and unexplored facets of the self. This exploration, rich in Norse magikal tradition, requires both dedication and patience. Here, we delve into practical exercises designed to deepen your connection with the dream world, employing techniques that blend ancient wisdom with modern practices, all while invoking the guidance of Freya and Frigg.

Dream Journaling: The Foundation of Dreamwork
Creating Your Sacred Journal

Start by selecting a journal that resonates with you, one that feels like a sacred vessel for your dreams. It could be adorned with symbols of Freya and Frigg or something simple that feels naturally connected to your spirit. Dedicate this journal to your dreamwork by performing a small ritual: light a candle (preferably white or silver), place a few drops of lavender oil on the journal for clarity and calm, and recite a dedication:

"Freya and Frigg, guides in the night, bless this journal with your insight. May the dreams within these pages hold the wisdom of the ages."

Daily Practice

Each night before sleep, write a small intention in your journal, something like, "Tonight, I journey through the dreamscape under the watchful eyes of Freya and Frigg." This sets a purposeful tone for your subconscious explorations.

Tips for Dream Recall

Pre-Sleep Ritual

Create a pre-sleep ritual to signal to your mind that you're ready to remember your dreams. This could involve lighting a specific incense (sandalwood works well for its calming properties), placing a moonstone under your pillow for intuition, or simply meditating for a few minutes on the intention to recall your dreams.

Upon Waking

As soon as you wake, remain still and keep your eyes

closed. In this tranquil state, try to grasp the threads of your dreams. Do not worry about the narrative making sense; just focus on any image, emotion, or word that comes to mind.

Recording Dreams

Write down everything you remember in your journal. If the dream is unclear, jot down any feelings or moods you experienced. Over time, patterns may emerge that are significant in your magikal practice.

Engaging with Freya and Frigg in Dreams

Visualization Exercise

Before sleep, visualize a meeting place in your dreams where you can converse with Freya and Frigg. This could be a Norse temple or a serene forest. Imagine yourself there, speaking with the goddesses and seeking their wisdom.

Dream Incubation

This is a technique where you focus on a specific question or problem before sleep, asking Freya and Frigg for guidance. Write your query in your journal and meditate on it before sleeping, with the expectation that the answer or guidance will come through in your dreams.

Interpreting Dreams

Symbolic Language

Dreams speak in the language of symbols. When interpreting your dreams, consider the symbolic meanings of the elements present, especially those related to Norse mythology or aspects of Freya and Frigg. For instance, a falcon might represent a message from Freya.

Further dream analysis is beyond the scop of this book, so I suggested you seek out more on dreams.

Intuitive Analysis

Trust your intuition in interpreting dreams. Sometimes, what seems nonsensical to the conscious mind holds profound meaning for the subconscious. Let your intuition guide you to understand the hidden messages.

Advanced Practice: Lucid Dreaming

Lucid Dreaming Techniques

To achieve lucidity – the state of being aware that you're dreaming – practice reality checks throughout the day, like reading a sentence, looking away, and then reading it again. In dreams, text often changes, and this habit can trigger lucidity.

Honestly, space prevents me from going into greater depth on this topic, but there are plenty of online resources on

Lucid Dreaming.

Meeting Freya and Frigg

Once you achieve lucidity, call upon Freya and Frigg within your dream. They may appear to you, offering guidance or knowledge that can aid your magikal practices and personal growth.

Incorporating Freya and Frigg into your dreamwork bridges the gap between the conscious and subconscious realms, providing a wellspring of insight and empowerment. Remember, the key to successful dreamwork lies in patience and persistence. Over time, this practice will deepen your connection to the Norse goddesses, enriching both your magikal and personal journey.

Working with dreams and the subconscious in Norse magik is an art that opens up a world of self-discovery and insight. It's a journey that takes one deep into the realms of their own mind, guided by the wisdom of Freya and Frigg, and empowered by the rich traditions of Norse sorcery.

As we move from this exploration of the inner mind, we transition into the ancient and potent practice of rune work, another key aspect of Norse magik that offers its own unique pathways to understanding and power.

Runes and Rune Casting

Within the enchanting world of Norse magic, the runes emerge as age-old symbols embodying immense power and unfathomable mystery. These enigmatic symbols, each a key to universal truths and cosmic forces, offer a path to understanding and influencing the world's intricate web. The use of runes in Norse magikal practices is not merely a method of divination, but a profound way to engage with the primal energies of the universe, with each rune serving as a conduit for specific energies and intentions.

Understanding runes begins with familiarizing oneself with each symbol's meaning and significance. The Elder Futhark, the oldest form of the runic alphabet, consists of 24 runes, each embodying a unique aspect of existence – from tangible concepts like wealth and protection to more abstract ideas like joy and mystery. For instance, Fehu, representing wealth and abundance, can be used in spells for prosperity, while Algiz, symbolizing protection, is ideal for warding rituals.

Incorporating runes into magikal practices requires a respectful and mindful approach. One must not only understand the meanings of the runes but also how to combine them to create harmonious and powerful spells. Each rune combination is a carefully crafted recipe, with the runes working together to create a specific magikal effect.

Simple Exercise: Rune Casting for Guidance
Materials:

A set of runes, traditionally carved in wood, stone, or bone.

A cloth or mat to cast the runes on.

A quiet and comfortable space for reflection.

Steps:

Preparation: Begin by grounding yourself. Take deep breaths and center your mind, focusing on your intention to seek guidance from the runes.

Casting the Runes: Gently mix the runes in their bag or container. With your question or intention in mind, draw three runes and cast them onto the cloth.

Interpreting the Runes: Observe the runes that have appeared. The first rune represents the current situation, or the root of your question. The second rune provides insight into the challenges or factors influencing the situation. The third rune suggests a potential outcome or course of action.

Reflection: Spend time reflecting on the meanings of the runes and how they relate to each other and your situation. Consider writing down your thoughts and interpretations in a journal.

Closing the Ritual: Thank the runes for their guidance. Store them respectfully until their next use.

This exercise in rune casting is a fundamental practice in Norse magik, providing insights and answers to practitioners. It allows for a deeper engagement with the ancient wisdom of the runes, opening pathways of understanding and personal growth.

In addition to divination, runes can also be incorporated into other magikal workings. Engraving or painting runes onto candles, amulets, or talismans can imbue these objects with specific energies. For example, engraving Raidho, a rune associated with travel and movement, on a travel amulet, can provide protection and ensure a smooth journey.

Runes can also be used in meditation and visualization practices. Focusing on a specific rune while meditating can help internalize its energies and teachings, allowing for a deeper connection with the rune's power.

The use of runes in Norse magikal practices is a multifaceted discipline, offering pathways to divination, spell work, and personal enlightenment. I hope I have given you a nice peek into the mysteries of the runes, providing you with a comprehensive understanding of these ancient symbols and practical ways to incorporate them into their magikal practices. As you explore the profound depths of rune magik, you find yourself not only tapping into the ancient wisdom of the Norse but also unlocking your own inner potentials and insights.

CHAPTER 13

Embracing Duality: The Balance Between Freya and Frigg

In the nuanced realm of Norse magik, the interplay of love and knowledge, as depicted by the goddesses Freya and Frigg, is a tapestry of profound complexity and beauty. Let' do a run through to attempt to understand this intricate dance between love, often associated with Freya, and knowledge, a realm presided over by Frigg. This exploration is not just about distinguishing these domains, but also about appreciating how they intertwine and complement each other in the practice of magik.

Imagine magik as a river, flowing through the landscape of the Norse spiritual world. On one bank of this river stands Freya, her presence radiating love, passion, and fertility. She embodies the heart's desires, the visceral emotional connections that bind us to each other and to the world. Love, in Freya's domain, is not just a feeling but a force, a magikal current that

154

inspires, transforms, and energizes.

Across the river stands Frigg, her essence imbued with wisdom, foresight, and understanding. She symbolizes the mind's pursuit, the quest for knowledge and insight. Frigg's realm is one of strategic thought, intuition, and the profound understanding of the world's mysteries. Knowledge, in her hands, is not merely information but a tool for navigating life's complexities, a guiding light in the world of magik.

The magik in understanding the interplay of love and knowledge lies in recognizing that these forces are not separate but are, in fact, two sides of the same coin. Love without knowledge can be aimless and untamed, while knowledge without love can be cold and disconnected. In magik, these elements must be balanced and harmonized, allowing the practitioner to tap into a more holistic and potent form of power.

Integrating the qualities of both goddesses into one's magikal practice involves embracing both the emotional depth of Freya and the intellectual acumen of Frigg. It means engaging in rituals and spells with both heart and mind, ensuring that every magikal act is as informed as it is impassioned. For example, a love spell guided by Freya's energy should also consider the wisdom of Frigg – understanding the broader consequences and the deeper needs that such a spell addresses.

This balance is also reflected in the way one approaches learning and growth in magik. It's about pursuing knowledge with passion and engaging with emotions intelligently. It's about allowing intuition and logic to guide one's path in equal measure. The practitioner who walks this balanced path understands that true magikal mastery comes from the harmonious union of love and knowledge.

In summary, the interplay of love and knowledge in magik, as embodied by Freya and Frigg, is a dance of dual forces, each enriching and enhancing the other. As we move forward in this chapter, we will explore how to integrate the qualities of both goddesses into practice, weaving their energies together to create a more nuanced and powerful approach to Norse magik and spirituality. This exploration is not just an academic exercise, but a journey to the heart of what it means to be a practitioner of Norse magik, where the balance of love and knowledge is the key to unlocking true magikal potential.

Access Both Goddesses At Once

I get questions, and one common question is, can one combine the power of two beings in the same ritual?

The answer is an unqualified yes.

I combine spirits all the time. Just recently, I worked some family magik for a client using both Aphrodite and Lilith. Their energies just meshed well together. I used the goddess aspect of Lilith, and her goddess sigil, with the sigil I'd made for Aphrodite.

The results were quite powerful.

With this in mind, integrating the qualities of both Freya and Frigg into practice is akin to harmonizing two powerful but distinct melodies into a single symphonic masterpiece. Let's investigate the art of blending the passionate, emotive energy of Freya with the wise, intuitive essence of Frigg, creating a balanced and holistic magikal practice. The journey of integrating these divine attributes is not just about invoking their powers, but about embodying their qualities, allowing them to guide and shape your spiritual path.

Imagine your magikal practice as a garden – a sacred space where different energies bloom and intertwine. In one corner, the flowers of Freya grow – wild, vibrant, and full of passion. These blooms represent love, desire, and the raw energy of life itself. Tending to this part of the garden involves engaging with your emotions, understanding your deepest desires, and using that understanding to fuel your magikal work.

In another corner of this garden, the herbs of Frigg flourish – wise, fragrant, and imbued with deep knowledge. These herbs symbolize insight, foresight, and the power of the mind. Tending to this part of the garden means cultivating your intuition, seeking knowledge, and applying that wisdom to your practices.

The key to integrating the qualities of Freya and Frigg lies in understanding when to draw upon each goddess's energy.

When casting a spell for love or passion, invoke Freya's energy, but temper it with Frigg's wisdom, ensuring that your actions are guided by insight and not just impulse. Similarly, when seeking knowledge or understanding, call upon Frigg's essence, but infuse it with Freya's vitality to ensure that your pursuit of wisdom is also a pursuit of personal growth and fulfillment.

Rituals and spells that blend both energies can be particularly potent. For instance, a ritual for emotional healing might begin with invoking Freya, asking for her assistance in opening and healing the heart. This can be followed by a prayer to Frigg, seeking her guidance in understanding and learning from the emotional journey. This melding of energies creates a magikal working that is both deeply healing and profoundly insightful.

Another aspect of integrating these goddesses into your practice recognizes and honoring the duality within yourself. Acknowledge that you, too, possess both emotional depth and intellectual strength. Embrace the passion and intuition, the love and knowledge that reside within you. Let your magikal practices reflect this inner duality, a celebration of the complex and multifaceted nature of your spirit.

Incorporating the qualities of Freya and Frigg into your daily life is also essential. This might involve simple acts like starting your day with a meditation that honors both love and wisdom or keeping symbols of both goddesses on your altar as a reminder of their balanced energies. It could also involve studying the myths and stories of Freya and Frigg, seeking within them lessons and insights that apply to your life and practice.

Integrating the qualities of Freya and Frigg into your magikal practice is about more than just invoking their powers; it's about weaving their essences into the very fabric of your spiritual journey. As we explore this integration, we not only enrich our understanding of Norse magik but also deepen our connection to these powerful goddesses, learning to walk a path that honors both the heart and the mind. This part of the chapter offers practical insights and guidance on this journey, encouraging the reader to embrace the duality within and to harness the combined powers of love and knowledge in their magikal practices.

Sample Ritual Incorporating Freya and Frigg

This ritual harmonizes the energies of Freya and Frigg, blending love and wisdom to empower any magikal working. By invoking these deities, the practitioner taps into Freya's passionate strength and Frigg's insightful foresight, creating a balanced and potent force. This ritual can be adapted to various intentions, inviting the reader to apply it to their specific needs.

Materials Needed:

Two Altar Candles: One green (for Freya) and one blue

(for Frigg).

Figurines or Sigils of Freya and Frigg: To represent and invoke the goddesses.

Incense: Preferably sandalwood for grounding and clarity.

A Bowl of Water: Symbolizing emotional intuition and clarity.

A Small Cloth Bag: To create a talisman.

Crystals: Rose quartz (for Freya) and clear quartz (for Frigg).

Offerings: Honey or mead for Freya, and bread or herbs for Frigg.

Paper and Pen: To write down your intention.

Ritual Steps:

Prepare Your Space: Arrange the altar with the green and blue candles, the figurines or symbols of Freya and Frigg, and the bowl of water. Place the incense in a holder near the altar.

Cleansing: Light the incense to cleanse the area, allowing its aroma to purify the space and your mind.

Setting the Intention: Write down your specific intention on the paper. Fold it and place it in the small cloth bag, along with the rose quartz and clear quartz.

Lighting the Candles: Light the green candle for Freya and the blue candle for Frigg, acknowledging their presence and inviting their energies into your space.

Invocation Prayer:

"Freya and Frigg, goddesses divine,

In love and wisdom, let our energies entwine.

Freya, bring your passion and might,

Frigg, guide with your insight so bright.

Together, empower this magikal rite."

Offerings: Place your offerings before the figurines or symbols of the goddesses. As you do so, express your gratitude and speak your intention aloud.

Charging the Talisman: Hold the cloth bag with the crystals and intention paper. Visualize your intention being empowered by the combined energies of Freya and Frigg. Feel the blend of love and wisdom infusing the talisman.

Sealing the Ritual: Thank Freya and Frigg for their guidance and blessings. Extinguish the candles, starting with Freya's and then Frigg's.

After the Ritual: Keep the talisman with you or place it in a significant area to remind you of your intention and the combined powers of Freya and Frigg.

Disposing of Offerings: Respectfully dispose of the offerings by returning them to nature or consuming them if appropriate.

This ritual is a powerful way to harness the complementary energies of Freya and Frigg, creating a harmonious balance of emotional depth and intellectual insight in your magikal workings. It invites us to experience the potency of integrating love and knowledge, opening the door to limitless possibilities in their spiritual journey.

The Concept of Duality in Norse Magik

In the intricate world of Norse magik and spirituality, the concept of duality is not only essential but deeply enigmatic. It's a theme woven into the very fabric of Norse cosmology, where opposing forces and contrasting energies coexist, creating a dynamic and harmonious balance. This part of the chapter explores the concept of duality within Norse magik, unraveling how this principle permeates the Norse spiritual landscape, shaping its myths, deities, and magikal practices.

At the heart of Norse spirituality lies the concept that opposites are not conflicting forces, but complementary ones. This is evident in the very structure of the Norse cosmos, where worlds like Muspelheim (the realm of fire) and Niflheim (the realm of ice) exist in opposition, yet their interaction leads to the creation of life. In this cosmic dance, duality is not about conflict but about the interplay of energies that gives birth to existence and evolution.

This principle of duality extends to the Norse pantheon, where gods and goddesses embody contrasting aspects. Freya and Frigg, for instance, represent different facets of femininity. Freya, with her passionate and fiery nature, symbolizes aspects of love, sensuality, and fertility. In contrast, Frigg, embodying wisdom, foresight, and the hearth, represents the nurturing, intuitive, and intellectual aspects. Together, they form a complete picture, reflecting the full spectrum of feminine energy in Norse spirituality.

Duality in Norse magik is also reflected in the understanding of life and death, light and shadow, chaos and order. Norse rituals and spells often acknowledge and invoke these dual aspects. For instance, a spell for protection may call upon the fierce, combative energy of Thor while also seeking the protective, nurturing care of Frigg. In this way, Norse magik recognizes that strength and vulnerability, action and reflection are equally vital in achieving balance and efficacy in magikal workings.

Moreover, the concept of duality in Norse spirituality teaches the practitioner the importance of balance within themselves. It encourages embracing both the light and shadow aspects of one's personality. Understanding and integrating these aspects is crucial for personal growth and spiritual development. A practitioner who recognizes and honors their own duality is better equipped to navigate the complexities of life and the challenges of magikal practice.

In practical terms, working with the concept of duality in Norse magik involves creating rituals and spells that honor and balance opposing energies. This could mean performing a ritual that celebrates both the end and the beginning, such as acknowledging the death of the old year and the birth of the new at Winter Solstice. It might also involve spells that draw upon both aggressive and defensive energies for protection or healing work that addresses both the physical and emotional aspects of the ailment.

In essence, the concept of duality within Norse magik and spirituality is a powerful reminder of the interconnectedness of all things. It teaches that opposites are not inherently antagonistic but are aspects of a greater whole that must be understood and honored. This understanding of duality provides a rich and nuanced framework for Norse magikal practices, offering a path to a more balanced and holistic approach to spirituality.

CHAPTER 14

Pathworking Freya and Frigg

Within the intricate and multifaceted realm of Norse magik, Pathworking emerges as an extraordinary and deeply meaningful technique, serving as a transformative expedition across the vast landscapes of the subconscious mind, facilitating a direct and profound interaction with divine energies and archetypes., Pathworking stands as a unique and profound practice, a journey through the realms of the subconscious to engage directly with divine energies and archetypes. This part of the chapter illuminates the concept of Pathworking, unraveling its mysteries and revealing its transformative potential. Pathworking is not just a method of spiritual exploration; it is an odyssey into the deeper aspects of the self, guided by the energies of deities like Freya and Frigg.

At its core, Pathworking is a guided meditation or visualization technique, where the practitioner embarks on a mental and spiritual journey, traversing various paths or realms within their mind. Imagine Pathworking as a journey through an intricate labyrinth, where each turn and corridor leads to new insights, encounters with divine beings, and deeper understanding of one's own psyche. The purpose of this practice is manifold: it serves as a tool for self-discovery, a method for obtaining guidance or wisdom, and a way to deepen one's connection with the divine.

The power of Pathworking lies in its ability to tap into the subconscious mind, where symbols and archetypes reside. By engaging with these symbols in a controlled and conscious way, practitioners can unlock new levels of awareness and understanding. In Norse magik, Pathworking often involves journeys to realms inhabited by gods and goddesses, engaging with them to gain their insights and blessings.

When Pathworking with Freya, the journey is one of passion, strength, and transformation. Freya's realm is vibrant and alive with her energies of love, fertility, and magikal prowess. A Pathworking journey with Freya might involve traversing a lush, green forest or walking through her magnificent hall, Sessrúmnir. In this journey, you may encounter Freya in her various aspects - as a lover, a warrior, or a sorceress. Engaging with Freya in Pathworking allows for a deep exploration of one's own desires, strengths, and magikal abilities. It can be a journey of empowerment, love, or even self-discovery.

Pathworking with Frigg, on the other hand, is a journey of wisdom, foresight, and nurturing. A journey with Frigg might take you through the clouds to her hall, Fensalir, a place of tranquility and insight. In this journey, you may engage with Frigg as the all-knowing mother, the weaver of fates, or the protector of homes. This Pathworking can be a quest for wisdom, an exploration of your own intuitive abilities, or a search for guidance in matters of the home and family.

In both forms of Pathworking, the practitioner engages in a dialogue – either literal or symbolic – with the deity. This engagement is not a passive experience; it requires active participation, where the practitioner asks questions, seeks guidance, and receives insights. The journey is often concluded with a gesture of gratitude to the deity, acknowledging the wisdom or guidance received.

Pathworking is a versatile practice that can be tailored to any purpose. Whether seeking guidance, strength, love, or wisdom, the practitioner can craft their journey to align with their intention. It is a practice that combines imagination, intuition, and spiritual exploration, making it a powerful tool in the hands of a skilled practitioner.

Pathworking Freya

A Pathworking journey with Freya, the Norse goddess of

love, war, and magik, is to traverse a landscape rich in symbolism and profound meaning. I now invite you on a vivid exploration through the realms of Freya, presenting a series of images that not only captivate the mind but also engage the heart and soul. Each image in this journey is designed to unlock different facets of Freya's power, helping practitioners of all levels to harness her energies for any purpose they seek.

1. The Enchanted Forest of Freya

Your journey begins in an ethereal forest, where the trees whisper ancient secrets, and the air is thick with magik. This is Freya's domain, a place where her energies of fertility, growth, and natural intuition are most potent. As you walk through this forest, you feel a deep connection to the earth and the life it sustains. The vibrant greenery and the chorus of wildlife around you are manifestations of Freya's vibrant life force. Here, you are reminded of the interconnectedness of all living things and Freya's role as a nurturer and sustainer.

2. The Hall of Sessrúmnir

Emerging from the forest, you find yourself in front of Sessrúmnir, Freya's majestic hall. This grand structure, resplendent and welcoming, is where Freya's aspect as a leader and protector shines. As you enter the hall, you're enveloped in an aura of warmth and strength. The hall is a space of sanctuary, a reminder of Freya's protective nature. Here, amidst the laughter and camaraderie of Freya's chosen warriors, you find courage and companionship. This is a place to gather strength, to seek Freya's guidance in matters of conflict, or to find solace in times of need.

3. The Seiðr Chamber

Deeper within Sessrúmnir lies a dimly lit chamber, the heart of Freya's seiðr magik. In this sacred space, illuminated by flickering candlelight, the air is thick with the essence of divination and foresight. Here, Freya's power of prophecy and her mastery of fate are most accessible. This chamber invites you to explore the mysteries of the unknown, to seek answers and understanding beyond the veil of the mundane world. It's a space for deep introspection and revelation, where the threads of fate can be unraveled and woven anew.

4. The Falcon's Aerie

Your final vision in this Pathworking journey with Freya is a high mountain peak, where the sky meets the earth. Here, you stand at the Falcon's Aerie, a place that symbolizes Freya's freedom and perspective. As you gaze out from this lofty height, you embody the spirit of the falcon, one of Freya's sacred animals. This vantage point offers a broader perspective on life, encouraging you to rise above daily concerns and see the bigger picture. In this moment, you are aligned with Freya's visionary aspect, empowered to see your life and your path with clarity and insight.

Each of these vivid images in your Pathworking journey with Freya serves a unique purpose. They are not just visualizations, but portals to different aspects of Freya's divine energy. As you engage with these images, you connect more deeply with her essence, drawing upon her strengths to empower your own magikal and spiritual practices.

Pathworking with Freya for any purpose is a journey of discovery and empowerment. It allows you to explore various aspects of her divine nature and to integrate her energies into your life. This journey is not just a practice of visualization; it is an immersive experience that weaves Freya's power into the fabric of your being, transforming and enlightening you in profound ways. As I move forward in this chapter, the journey continues, revealing how to similarly engage with Frigg in Pathworking, thus enriching your spiritual practice with the wisdom and power of another revered Norse deity.

Pathworking Frigg

Pathworking with Frigg, the Norse goddess of wisdom, foresight, and the hearth, is a journey through a realm where deep intuition and maternal insight reign supreme. This section invites you to embark on a pathworking adventure with Frigg, guiding you through a series of vivid, symbolic landscapes that capture her essence. Each image is a gateway into understanding Frigg's multifaceted nature, providing insights and lessons relevant to any purpose or intention you bring to your practice.

1. The Hearth of Fensalir

Your pathworking journey begins in Fensalir, Frigg's beloved hall, known for its warmth and sanctuary. Here, you find yourself in a cozy room where a fire crackles in the hearth, casting a gentle, welcoming glow. This space symbolizes the heart of the home and family, where Frigg's nurturing and protective energies are most potent. As you sit by the fire, you feel enveloped in a sense of peace and security. This is a place for reflection on familial bonds, for seeking guidance on matters of the home, or for simply basking in the comfort of Frigg's maternal love.

2. The Loom of Destiny

Moving deeper into Fensalir, you come upon a grand room where Frigg stands before a magnificent loom. The threads she weaves are not mere yarn but the very strands of fate itself. Here, in the presence of the loom, you are invited to contemplate the tapestry of your life. Each thread represents a different aspect of your existence – choices made, paths taken, relationships formed. This image teaches you about the interconnectedness of actions and consequences and offers insight into how your choices weave the fabric of your destiny.

3. The Cloudy Vistas

Next, your journey takes you above Fensalir, to the realms of clouds and sky where Frigg's vision extends across the Nine Worlds. Standing atop a cloud, you gaze upon the vastness of the world below. This vantage point symbolizes Frigg's foresight and wisdom. From here, you can see the broader picture of your life and the world around you. This perspective encourages strategic thinking, planning, and the understanding that every action is part of a larger whole. It is a reminder of the power of foresight and the importance of looking beyond the immediate.

4. The Sacred Grove

Your pathworking with Frigg concludes in a sacred grove, a tranquil place of deep spiritual connection. Here, amidst ancient trees and a gently flowing stream, you find a space for quiet meditation and introspection. This grove is a symbol of inner wisdom and spiritual insight. In this serene setting, you are encouraged to connect with your inner self, to listen to the quiet voice of intuition that Frigg embodies. It is a place for finding inner peace, for gaining clarity on your spiritual path, and for connecting with the deeper, often overlooked aspects of your psyche.

Each of these vivid pathworking scenes with Frigg offers a unique perspective on her divine qualities. They are not just visualizations but experiential realms where you can interact with the goddess's energy, learning from her wisdom and incorporating her insights into your practice. Whether seeking guidance in familial matters, understanding the paths of destiny, gaining strategic foresight, or connecting with inner wisdom, these pathworking journeys provide a rich, immersive experience into the heart of Frigg's power.

In conclusion, pathworking with Frigg for any purpose is an exploration of the depths of wisdom, intuition, and spiritual insight. It is a journey that strengthens the connection between the practitioner and the divine, empowering them with the knowledge and understanding that Frigg so gracefully embodies. As this chapter progresses, these pathworking experiences lay the foundation for a deeper, more profound engagement with Norse magik and spirituality, enriching your practice with the nurturing wisdom of one of its most revered goddesses.

CHAPTER 15

As we draw the curtains on this enlightening journey through the mystical landscapes of Norse magik, it is time to gather the rich tapestry of lessons and practices we have explored. This final part of this book is a reflective pool, mirroring the key teachings of Freya and Frigg, and offering insights on how to weave their wisdom into the fabric of our daily lives. Here, we summarize the profound lessons imparted by these goddesses, crystallizing their essence into tangible practices that can illuminate our personal magikal journeys.

Summarizing Key Lessons and Practices

Our exploration began with understanding the distinct yet complementary powers of Freya and Frigg. Freya, the embodiment of love, beauty, and war, taught us the art of channeling passion, embracing strength, and the intricacies of seiðr magik. Her lessons extend beyond the realms of love and war, teaching us about the vitality of life and the power of transformation. The practices centered around Freya showed us how to harness our desires and turn them into magikal intentions, how to stand strong in the face of adversity, and how to tap into the primal forces of nature for empowerment.

Frigg, on the other hand, offered a journey into the realms of wisdom, foresight, and nurturing. Through her, we learned the value of intuition, the importance of protecting what we cherish, and the art of looking beyond the surface to understand the deeper truths of life. Frigg's teachings are a reminder of the power of inner knowledge, the strength in quiet understanding, and the importance of foreseeing the consequences of our actions.

Incorporating the Teachings into Daily Life

Integrating the wisdom of Freya and Frigg into daily life is about recognizing and honoring the duality within us and the world around us. It involves acknowledging our emotional depth as well as our intellectual insights. In practical terms, this could mean starting each day with a moment of gratitude, a ritual that honors both love (Freya) and wisdom (Frigg). It might involve setting intentions for the day that balance our desires with our responsibilities, or it could be as simple as acknowledging the beauty and the lessons in our everyday experiences.

Creating an altar or sacred space that reflects the energies of both goddesses can serve as a daily reminder of their teachings. This space can be a focal point for meditation, reflection, and connection with the divine. Additionally, practicing mindfulness and being present in our interactions, whether with nature, other people, or ourselves, can be a way of embodying the goddesses' wisdom.

A Final Blessing and Continuation of Personal Magikal Journeys

As we conclude this chapter, let us invoke a final blessing from Freya and Frigg:

"May the passion and strength of Freya guide your heart,
And the wisdom and foresight of Frigg enlighten your path.
In their balance, find your power,
In their teachings, see life's flower."

This journey through the Norse magik of Freya and Frigg is not an end but a beginning. It's an invitation to continue exploring, learning, and growing in your magikal practice. The lessons and practices outlined here are steppingstones, gateways to deeper understanding and personal evolution. As you move forward, carry the wisdom of the goddesses with you, let their energies inspire and shape your path, and may your journey be as rich and fulfilling as the magik you weave.

GLOSSARY

Algiz: A rune symbolizing protection and defense in Norse magik.

Brisingamen: Freya's famed necklace, a token of beauty and charm, and a source of her magikal might.

Elder Futhark: The oldest form of the runic alphabets, consisting of 24 runes, each embodying a unique aspect of existence.

Falcon's Aerie: A symbolic place in Freya's pathworking, representing freedom and perspective.

Fehu: A rune representing wealth and abundance.

Fensalir: Frigg's hall, a symbol of tranquility, wisdom, and maternal insight.

Frigg: Norse goddess of wisdom, foresight, and the hearth.

Freya: Norse goddess of love, beauty, war, and magik.

Goddesses: Deities in Norse mythology, central to various practices and beliefs.

Hall of Sessrúmnir: Freya's grand hall, symbolizing her protective and nurturing nature.

Loom of Destiny: A symbolic tool in Frigg's realm representing fate and life's interconnectedness.

Magik: Practices and beliefs involving the manipulation of mystical or supernatural forces.

Norse Magik: The specific magikal practices and beliefs derived from Norse mythology and spirituality.

Pathworking: A guided meditation or visualization technique used in spiritual practices to engage with divine energies and archetypes.

Raidho: A rune associated with travel and movement.

Runic: Pertaining to runes, the ancient alphabetic script used for writing, divination, and magikal purposes in Norse and Germanic cultures.

Seiðr: An ancient form of Norse magik often associated with prophecy and altering fate.

Sessrúmnir: Freya's hall in Norse mythology, a symbol of her protective and nurturing nature.

Subconscious: The part of the mind that is not fully conscious but influences actions and feelings.

Valkyries: Mythological figures in Norse culture, choosers of the slain in battle, associated with Freya.

Wisdom: An important attribute in Norse spirituality, often associated with Frigg.

Sigils

Freya

FREYA

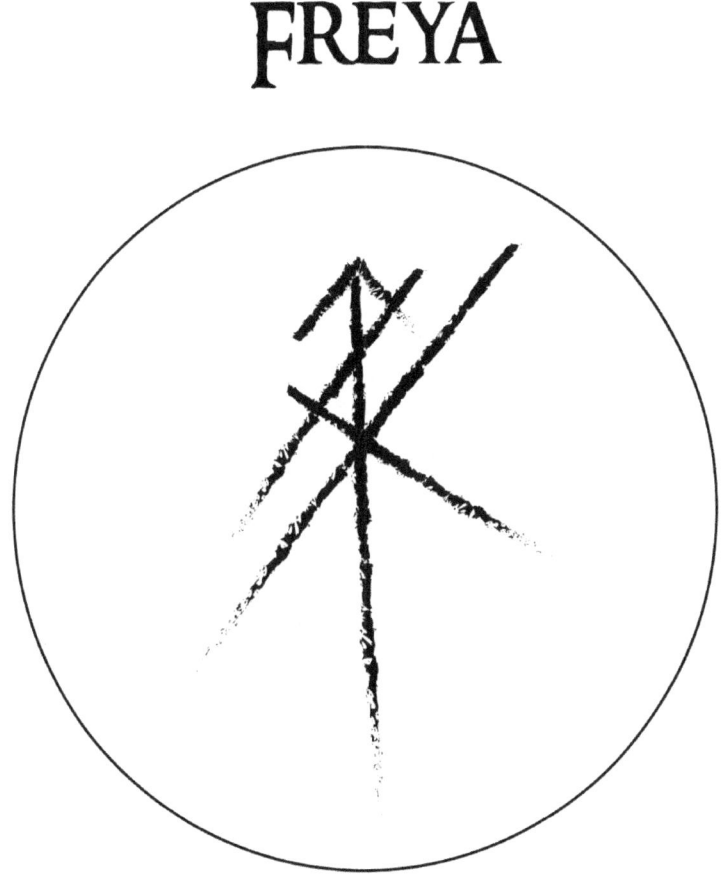

Frigg

FRIGG

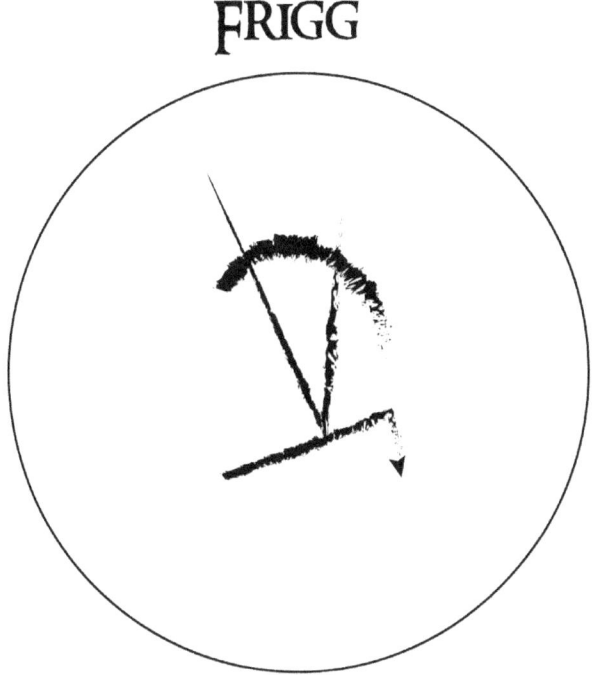

ABOUT THE AUTHOR

Dave is an author of adult fantasy (The Furies series) as well as author of occult books about magick.

He began working ritual magick back in the 1970s. He took a brief break, then used the power of this magick to create a photography career which took him to Los Angeles and work as a photographer for multiple magazines.

David has studied magick in all forms, and in 2018, released a three-part magick instruction course in High Magick. Thousands of students have benefited from David's unique teaching style, making ceremonial magick accessible to everyone.

Dave also has a series on Grecian Magick, exploring the aspects of ceremonial magick with the gods and goddesses of ancient Greece.

Dave's Facebook Page:

https://www.facebook.com/DavePsychic/

Secrets of Magick Facebook Group:

https://www.facebook.com/groups/secretsofmagick

Join the Grecian Magick Facebook group!

https://www.facebook.com/groups/grecianmagick

Dave's webpage, book readings and his services:

https://davepsychic.com

Then his e-learning website for magik classes

https://highmagikacademy.com

Magick Books by David Thompson

Available as EPUB, Paperback and Hardcover (*)

High Magick Series

- High Magick 101
- Daemons of High Magick
- Daemons and the Law of Attraction*
- Magick of Astaroth*
- Lilith: Goddess of Darkness and Light*
- Daemons of Fortune*
- Asmodeus King of Daemons*
- Goddesses of High Magick
- Protection Magik
- The Diviner's Handbook
- The Magik of Lucifer*
- The Magik of Freya and Frigg

Grecian Magick Series

- Magick of Apollo
- Magick of Hermes
- Magick of Aphrodite
- Magick of Fortuna*
- Greco-Roman Wealth Magick*
- Magick of the Sirens/Magick of the Muses
- Hermes and the Akashic Records

Fiction Novels by David Thompson

The Furies Series

- Angels of Vengeance
- Descent into Tartarus
- Furies: Beginnings
- Brianna: Making of a Fury